RON HUTCHCRAFT

TEN TIME BOMBS

Defusing the Most Explosive Pressures Teenagers Face

ZONDERVAN™

GRAND RAPIDS, MICHIGAN 49530

ZONDERVAN™

Ten Time Bombs
Copyright © 1997 by Ronald Hutchcraft

Requests for information should be addressed to:

Zondervan, *Grand Rapids, Michigan 49530*

Library of Congress Cataloging-in-Publication Data

Hutchcraft, Ronald.
    Ten time bombs: defusing the most explosive pressures teenagers face /
Ron Hutchcraft.
        p.   cm.
    ISBN: 0-310-20808-4
    1. Teenagers—Religious life. 2. Teenagers—Conduct of life.
3. Christian life—Juvenile literature. I. Title.
BV4531.2.H848 1997
248.8'3—dc21   97-15024

Printed in the United States of America

04 05 06 /❖ DC/ 20 19 18 17

CONTENTS

INTRODUCTION

If you're like a lot of young people I know, reading a book may not be on your personal "Top 10 List." If you've got a few minutes of personal time, it seems more exciting to plug into a video or a TV program or stereo than it does to pick up a book. By the time your English teacher and history teacher and biology teacher get finished with you, your brain is fried and flashing a red warning sign that says, "Overload! No more information!"

But this book isn't about some poem a guy wrote a century ago or a battle some armies fought three hundred years ago—this one is about the only life you get and how to make it a life you'll never regret! It's straight talk about some of the most important, sometimes most confusing pressures in your life: your friends, your relationship with your family, sex, the things that make you angry, the things that make you depressed, the things that make you hurt. How you handle your feelings and choices in these areas will decide the kind of life you have for many, many years—and even for the next few months!

Why did I take time to write all this down? Because I've seen these pressures blow up so many young lives—like deadly time bombs. I have had the privilege of working closely with thousands of teenagers—and the pain of watching too many hurt or destroyed by these "ten time bombs." And because I get mail constantly from the listeners to my national radio program for young people, I am hearing all the time the "if only I had known's" of hurting lives. A lot of what I want to give you in the pages ahead is from all those young people.

Their experience can show you where the time bombs are on the road ahead—those mistakes that can wreck the things that matter most to you.

But there's an even better way to make the most of the one life you've got. Listen to the person who put you here—He is the *only* One who can see the whole picture. He's like the man in the traffic helicopter—He can see the messes ahead that we could never see.

The biggest single reason people end up disappointed and depressed is not because they don't listen to their teachers or their leaders, or even their parents—it's because they don't listen to their *Creator*. Thankfully, He wrote a book—the world's best-selling book, the Bible. In those pages is the mistake-proof, big-picture advice of God Himself! That's why we will also check out His perspective on the pressures you face.

Every young person, including you, lives with pressures that really are like time bombs. But you don't have to be a victim—if you know how to defuse the most explosive pressures teenagers face. These pages are your personal "Bomb Squad" manual, showing you some very practical ways to avoid life-wrecking explosions.

Your life can be dynamite if you know how to handle the bombs. You're about to find out how.

1 Sex at Its Best!

Sacrificing Sex at Its Best for Sex Too Soon

Five people in our family—three of them teenagers. Each one doing their own thing in a different room of the house. My Mission Impossible—somehow get them all together in the living room for some family time. Good luck!

But what's the first thing they do when that *Mission Impossible* theme starts? Light a match! So I do—to start a fire in our fireplace. Of course, first I secretly turn down the thermostat on this cold winter night. As the house is getting colder, the living room is getting warmer. One by one, every shivering member of the family drifts into the room muttering, "Man, is it cold in this house!"

I love our fireplace. But our son Brad probably loves the fireplace most. Fortunately, he has never reached the point where he wants a fire too much. Imagine if I came home some night and smelled smoke coming from Brad's room. I would be in a panic, and I *should* be in a panic—there's no fireplace upstairs!

"Brad, do you smell smoke up there?"

"Yup."

9

"Where's it coming from?"

"Well, Dad—you know how I love those fires?"

"Yeah ..."

"I decided to build a fire in my room."

"But, Brad, there's no fireplace in your room!"

Fire is nice—when it's in the right place. It makes you warm and cozy. But that same fire outside of the fireplace will burn you and destroy things that matter to you.

Just like the fire of sex.

Sex in its right place, in its right time will warm and beautify your life. But when you play with sex outside the fireplace it was made for, you get burned and irreplaceable treasures get destroyed.

So many young people are deciding to try the "fire" without the "fireplace" and, in the process, giving up more than they could ever imagine. Having sex too soon is one of those ten time bombs that can do serious damage to your future.

Designer Love

"What are sex and love going to mean to me?"

That is one of the most important questions a teenager can answer. The question is so personal that no one else can or should answer it for you. Your parents can't answer it for you (even though they would like to go out on your dates with you, if they could). Your church or synagogue can't answer it for you. And it's too personal for you to let any friends give you an answer. So much of your future love and happiness is wrapped up in whether or not you make the right choice about what sex will mean to you.

If you get it right, sex can give you a life full of closeness, caring, and ultimate relationship. If you get it wrong, you will end up—as all too many people found out too late—with disappointment, regrets, loneliness, and maybe even disease.

Now, it's obvious that what "everybody" is doing isn't working. Too many people are ending up feeling used, lonely, and disillusioned. And the relationships our "go for it!" world is producing tell us that something is messed up. There is one divorce for every new marriage in America these days. If you had a machine where every other product it made broke, wouldn't you get a new machine? Well, our dating-and-mating "machine" is manufacturing "lifetime" relationships in which every other one breaks! Any thinking young person can see that there must be something better than this rush to physical relationships.

So, where do you look for that "something better"? For some honest help that will keep you from making the mistakes that ruin sex and love?

How about checking with the inventor of sex and love? "Check with Madonna?" someone asks. No, neither Madonna nor any media sex symbol created sex. "Check with *Playboy* or *Hustler*?" Sorry, no magazine invented sex either.

The starting point to have sex at its best is this simple, maybe surprising, fact: God invented sex, and the Inventor knows best.

No one knows as much about sex and how it is meant to be as God does. It only makes sense. If you have a question about your Chevrolet, contact Chevrolet—

they made it. If you have a question about your Windows software, contact Microsoft—they made it. And if you want to know how to have the best of sex and love, find out what God says … He made it!

My friend Mel keeps his garden protected by having a fence around it. The fence isn't there to keep everyone from enjoying it. It's there to keep it protected from unwanted animal visitors.

That's why the Creator of sex put the fence of marriage around it—not to ruin it, but to protect it. In His "manual on life and love"—the Bible—God describes the place He designated to keep sex special: "Marriage should be honored by all, and the marriage bed kept pure" (Hebrews 13:4).

The Inventor of sex says He designed it to be kept inside the fence called marriage. Jesus Christ described sex at its best when He told us, "At the beginning of creation, God 'made them male and female.' 'For this reason a man will leave his father and mother and be united to his wife, and the two will become one flesh.' So they are no longer two, but one. Therefore what God has joined together, let man not separate" (Mark 10:6–9).

Jesus was describing what most of us really want deep down inside—a lifetime love we can count on with someone we are totally committed to and who is totally committed to us. And He said an important part of the love between them is a sexual bond they have never experienced with anyone else.

Marriage is the fireplace where sex belongs. When "two become one flesh" within the fireplace of married love, sex warms your life in a uniquely beautiful way. But just like fire, when you play with sex outside the fireplace of marriage, you get tragically burned. The winds of passion will take you farther than you ever planned to go, keep you longer than you ever planned to stay, and leave you in a place where you never wanted to end up.

When the Failure Rate for Condoms Is 100%

It used to be that even married couples were a little embarrassed to talk about condoms. Now everybody is talking about them, and they're selling them right up front in the drugstore with the bubble gum and the chocolate bars! In some places, schools are even handing them out to students like Band-Aids. It seems as if the community is assuming most kids will have sex, it's inevitable, so let's give them what they need to protect themselves.

The theory is that with a condom you can protect yourself from the consequences of sex outside of marriage: AIDS, sexually transmitted disease, or pregnancy. But these are only the selective consequences of premarital sex—the ones only some young people experience. Usually, you have heard about those consequences so much that you almost get dangerously immune to all the lectures. Many teenagers decide they will roll the dice anyway and say, "Hey, I'll take my chances. Those things probably won't happen to me." Everyone who ever got back a positive HIV test or pregnancy test thought the same thing.

A lot of people are telling you about these selective consequences. But, chances are, no one is telling you about the *universal* consequences of sex before marriage.

These are the consequences that happen to every person who has sex outside of marriage. No condom on earth can protect you from one of these universal consequences: damaging memories.

The Invasion of the Video Monsters!

"Do we have to?"

That was our son Brad's reaction whenever we pulled out the old family video of our trip to Alaska. For some reason, he wasn't excited about seeing himself again in all his twelve-year-old splendor. He was entering that phase when the "caterpillar" is starting to turn into a "butterfly"—and when most people are some "caterfly" or "butterpillar" intermediate life-form.

Also, the video has an abrupt ending—his fourteen-year-old brother Doug was using the camcorder and didn't know how to turn it off. Consequently, the picture is enough to make you seasick in your own living room as it races up and down over snowdrifts, boots, clouds, and unidentified flying objects. The reason Brad hates it is because the audio features his high-pitched twelve-year-old voice squeaking in frustration—"Doug! You're still filming!" Unfortunately for Brad, because it's on video, those precious memories will never go away.

Not all recorded memories are ones we want to replay. Especially when it comes to memories of physical relationships you had before you were married.

A result of sex that few people ever think about at the time—one that happens to every person who has sex outside God's fence—is *damaging memories*. Because sex was designed by God for one man with one woman in lifetime relationship, He made it so it creates powerful, long-lasting memories. But when you have sex outside of marriage, the video camera in your soul is still filming, recording indelible impressions. When you are making out or making love, you are making memories.

And those memories start playing back just when you don't want them to—in the intimacy of your sexual love with your husband or wife. At a time when you were meant to be thinking of only one person in the whole world, another relationship is invading the most intimate moments of your life. God designed sex so that each married couple would develop their own, never-before, never-like-this language of love with each other. But the replays of previous experiences introduce comparison, guilt, and mental adultery into what was supposed to be some of the most beautiful moments of your life.

Don't take sex outside the fireplace of marriage—when you do, you are making damaging memories that can spoil sex at its best.

You Threw It Out?

For a long time, our son Doug thought his grandmother had committed the unpardonable sin.

When I was a kid, I dug pop bottles out of a vacant lot, went to the corner store, got the deposit money for them, and spent it all on baseball cards. Many years later—long after pop bottles had turned to pop cans—Doug went into baseball card collecting big time. He invested like the Donald Trump of cardboard. He liked rare cards that could be turned into big bucks. Like the ones I had in my boyhood collection.

There was just one small problem. My mother—Doug's grandmother—threw them all out some years ago when we were moving. After much therapy, Doug has finally been able to forgive his grandmother. But the fact remains—she threw away something really valuable without even knowing it!

Lost treasure. It's sad—especially when it comes to what could have been sex and love at its best. Every night, somewhere in this country, young men and women are having sex before marriage—and, without knowing it, throwing away treasures that are very, very valuable. And like damaging memories, lost treasure is a consequence of sex outside God's fence that affects every person involved and that no condom on earth can protect you against.

How Sex Is Like Scotch Tape

One treasure you lose with unmarried sex is your bondability. You can see bondability when you stick a piece of tape to something like the side of a desk. It sticks. It stays. But take that same piece of tape and stick it on the floor, then several pieces of furniture, then a carpet—and finally on the side of the desk again. This time it won't stick. It won't stay. It has lost something important—its bondability.

When God created sex, He created it with bonding power, to glue two people together "till death do us part." No matter how casual or serious the relationship, inside or outside of marriage, sex *will* bond people as if this were a forever relationship. That's the way sex was created—you cannot make it *not* bond the two people involved. Speaking of the most meaningless sex of all, the Designer says, "Do you not know that he who unites himself with a prostitute is one with her in body? For it is said, 'The two will become one flesh'" (1 Corinthians 6:16).

That man bonded with that prostitute in the same way sex was supposed to bond him with his wife. Everytime you get sexually involved with someone, you are bonding, whether you realize it or not. And like that reused piece of tape, you are giving up a little of your bondability every time you have a sexual relationship. And that bondability is a treasure you will need as glue for your lifetime love. If you have bonded before you're married, you have used up some of your ability to give and receive real, lifetime love. No one is telling you that unmarried sex can cost you the precious treasure of your bondability. No one, that is, except the Inventor.

Maximum Excitement

Future trust is another treasure you can throw out as unknowingly as my mother threw out those valuable baseball cards. At the time your passions are pumping, you aren't thinking about what this might do to your marriage some day. But that consequence will last much longer than tonight's feelings of love. You won't realize until it's too late that tonight's "making love" is "trashing trust" for your future marriage.

You cannot have a stable marriage without trust— that confidence that you and your partner will have only each other sexually. That trust is what allows you to totally relax in your partner's love and experience sex at its best.

Before you're married, it's so easy to say, "Hey, who cares about the fence of marriage? After all, we love each other—isn't that all that matters?" So, you tear down the fence to have sex. The problem comes when you are later married to someone who did not think the fence was worth waiting for. So if the fence wasn't important enough to keep him or her out, how can you be sure it will be important enough to keep him or her in?

Bondability and your future partner's trust are treasures too valuable to trash. Beyond that, there is still another treasure you lose when the "fire" is "outside the fireplace."

The Excitement of the Unopened Gift

Christmas is always fun because of the excitement of the unopened gifts. Of course, we're all really curious about what's inside the beautifully wrapped packages, but to open them early can ruin Christmas. One year a young boy I know opened all his gifts two weeks before Christmas. On Christmas morning, instead of racing to the tree, he listlessly sat by and opened his gifts without much joy. "Are you sick?" his concerned parents asked. "No," he replied. "I just opened my gifts early and ruined Christmas!"

With sex, "Christmas" is your wedding night. The Inventor designed sex to be one man with one woman opening their gift inside a lifetime commitment to each other. Everything else is unnatural love. And God meant for it to be incredibly exciting and satisfying. He basically said that in His Book—"May you rejoice in the wife of your youth.... May her breasts satisfy you always, may you ever be captivated by her love" (Proverbs 5:18–19).

Now, someone will read that, get a curious look on their face, and ask, "Did God say that? Isn't that a little racy for God?" Of course not! He's the Inventor of sex! God thought up the male body, the female body, intercourse—it's all His idea. Once you're inside the fireplace of married love, God is saying, "Go for it!"

But what makes married love so exciting is that you have never loved anyone else in this way. There is an explosive excitement in knowing you have waited for each other, that you have a gift that you have saved exclusively for your lifetime lover. That is sex at its best!

God knows the frustration people experience when they love someone as they have never loved anyone else—but have nothing unique to give to say, "I love *you* forever!" They already gave it to someone else—and stole it from the one person who really should have gotten it. You can only give it the *first* time *one* time. God meant for it to be with your husband or wife.

In simple terms—it is worth the wait to have sex at its best.

The Sexual Secret You Need to Know

It's hard to think anything about sex is still a secret today, but there's one secret few people talk about. The ultimate unavoidable consequence of sex outside marriage is the *judgment of God*. His Word says, "For God will judge the adulterer and all the sexually immoral" (Hebrews 13:4).

One day we will stand before the One who gave us this wonder love-gift called sex and account for what we did with it. Society may not care if you have sex outside the fence, your family may never know, your feelings may tell you it's really okay, your friends may even congratulate you if you do, but your Creator has not changed His mind about sex and how He designed it to be!

God cares what you do with sex. He *knows* what you do with sex. He will never say it was okay outside of His marriage boundaries, and He will hold you accountable for what you do with His invention and the body He gave you. But judging you is never His first choice. He would rather forgive you—and before we finish, you will understand how that can happen.

With these universal consequences of damaging memories, lost treasure, and the judgment of God, how can you keep sex special? You need to have a plan.

Strategies for Keeping Sex Special

Sex at its best is for those who make the commitment—that whatever you have done before today—from today on, you will reserve sex for the person you marry. Once you decide that's what you want, you have to face a very important and practical question: "How am I going to keep sex special—especially when I'm surrounded by people who aren't, and with desires that keep pushing me to give in?"

Good question. It deserves some good answers.

God wants us to keep our bodies special, to reserve ourselves for the best. That's why He says, "You should avoid sexual immorality ... each of you should learn to control his own body" (1 Thessalonians 4:3–4).

Avoid—like you avoid a skunk with his tail in the air—don't get anywhere close to going too far. And *con-*

trol—like a campfire—do not let your passions get to the point where they could take over.

God knows the power He built into our sexual desires, and like a fire, that power is useful when it's in its place, but destructive when it gets outside its boundaries. We need an aggressive plan to avoid sex too soon and to control the sexual desires inside us—before they become a raging inferno!

Step 1: Decide Your Line in Advance

Unfortunately, most young people do not think about where they will stop until they are all wrapped around somebody. At that point, your glands are in control—and your glands disconnect your brain and your conscience. Waiting until you are almost out of control isn't exactly what the Inventor meant when He told us that each of you should learn to control your own body.

If you want an unforgettable—and expensive—object lesson on this, just take the family car out on the local expressway. Take it up to about seventy miles per hour and shift it into reverse! I hope you don't need the car again, and I hope you don't have to go home again. (Obviously, I don't advise this!)

What people would never try to do with a car, they try to do with their bodies all the time. They get it running fast and then suddenly try to reverse it! That is how so many people have gone so much farther than they ever planned to. They never thought ahead about the "top speed" they would allow their body to go in a romantic situation.

Of course, this leads to the most popular teenage question of all time—How far can I go?

The question is too important for a flip answer. Besides, it's the *wrong* question. To decide your "out of bounds," start with the *right* question: "How much do I want to have left for my lifetime love?"

When God gave us the desire for physical closeness with the opposite sex, He also gave us a *lot* of ways to show it—from holding hands to an arm around the shoulder, from a kiss to an embrace, from petting to intercourse. Your first line-drawing decision is how much of your love-expressions you want to reserve for your lifetime love. Anything you do with someone else, you are taking away from your life partner as an "exclusive." Don't be too quick to ask, "How far can I go?"

Any decision on your physical boundaries should take into account that sex is a package that includes the parts of your body that are involved in sexual love. The Designer says, "Do not offer the parts of your body to sin, as instruments of wickedness" (Romans 6:13).

The "parts of your body" that are sexual need to be totally reserved for your marriage partner. No one else should see or touch those "forever love" parts of you. When you are deciding your line, start there and work your way back, realizing you have a long run to the finish line.

When I was in high school, I had a savings account, briefly. I would get forty or fifty dollars in it, see something I wanted, and promptly crack open my nest egg. I cannot remember one thing I bought with that money. But I can remember what I wanted to buy, but couldn't—a car. "Oh, you didn't have enough money, huh?" Actually, I could have had enough money, but I blew it on all those impulsive, dinky purchases along the way. When the "big one" came along, I didn't have anything left to spend on it. I had spent it on every little thing that came along!

A lot of young people make that mistake with their physical affections. They keep using up their physical expressions of love on every little relationship along the way—and when the "big one" comes along, they have saved very little to spend on him or her.

That's why it is smart to open an "affection savings account." In it are all the ways you can physically express love to someone—from holding hands all the way up the chart to sexual intercourse. Certain expressions you decide right off will never be withdrawn until your wedding night. (Don't forget—a lot of engagements get broken. God says your bodies do not totally belong to each other until those public marriage commitments have been made!) Then, you start to work your way back, deciding certain expressions will not be withdrawn from your account until you are engaged, then farther back along the affection chart to a relationship where you have been going with the same person for several months.

The point is this: You make withdrawals from your account very carefully, and you don't throw away even the simplest expressions cheaply. Holding hands is not automatic just because you are out with someone—it has to mean something and only be withdrawn when there is a substantial reason. A kiss is not just a way to say "thank you for spending money on me." It has to mean something important. You cannot afford to waste any of your languages of love!

Why do you need to be so careful about affection withdrawals? Because you want to make it to the investment that really matters—your lifetime love—with a lot left to give.

If you have ever done any competitive running, you'll know the answer to this question—at what point in the race do you need the most resources? At the end! So, the champion learns the importance of something called *pacing*. It means you do not use up all your air and your energy early in the race. You're going to need the most resources as you get close to the finish line. Think about that when it comes to winning your run to sex at its best— you can't use up too much in the early laps of the race or you will not have enough left to make it to the finish line.

When it comes to expressing physical love, pacing means you make each love-expression meaningful and give it away very carefully.

One reason for that caution is a law of romantic relationships: You tend to start in your next relationship where you left off in your last relationship. That's understandable because this time you're sure it's *really* love. Most times it isn't. But let's say it took you a while to have a kissing-thing in relationship 1, then along comes relationship 2, and you will probably be into that kissing-thing right away. You escalate physically in each new relationship or as you keep going with someone longer and longer. The result for thousands of young people who wanted to keep sex special? They never made it to the finish line with the gifts they had meant to save. They gave too much too soon—and ultimately lost it all.

So drawing your physical line is one of the most important decisions you will make as a young person. Don't think of it as "How far can I go?" Think of it as "How much do I want to have left for my lifetime love?" The more you save, the more you will have to spend on a lifetime of love and pleasure.

Step 2: Declare Your Line

No matter where you stand on a football field, you can see where the boundaries are. If you're sitting up in the nosebleed section of the stadium, you can still see exactly where out of bounds is. A line is useless unless the players know where it is. So it's clearly marked in a thick, white line.

People need to know where your boundaries are. Your friends should know, and people you date should know, then you won't have as much pressure from people who are pushing to discover "how far he will go" or "how far she will go." And it will give courage to others either to set a high standard or keep the standard they have set.

Most important, it will strengthen your commitment to be on record with it. It gives you the accountability that helps you keep a commitment when you're pressured or weak. Don't be afraid to tell people that you have decided to keep sex special, you are keeping your gifts so you don't "ruin Christmas," and you have decided "the Inventor knows best."

"Weird!" Maybe you're afraid that's what people will think you are if you declare your line. Well, we need to go back to my son Doug's baseball card collection. He's got some cards that are worth many hundreds of dollars—they're rare rookie cards of some big stars. They are valuable because there are not many of them.

If you are committed to virginity, that does not make you weird. It makes you rare and valuable. In fact, the fewer people there are like you, the more valuable you become.

Step 3: Defend Your Line

You've decided it. You've declared it. Now you have to defend it. Let's face it, there are going to be lots of temptations and opportunities to compromise your line: an awesome guy or girl, lonely times, the fear of losing someone, happy hormones, the fatigue of being in the minority, feelings of love, and so on. You will be pushed and challenged over and over again before your wedding day. So you cannot just decide your boundaries. You have to actively defend them. And how do you do that? "Flee the evil desires of youth" (2 Timothy 2:22).

Notice the Inventor of sex doesn't say fight those wrong desires. He certainly doesn't say flirt with them. He tells us to flee them! I understand that. If you want to keep sex special, you don't get anywhere near situations where you could stumble. So, defending your line includes some very practical actions.

1. Limit the time you spend alone with someone you care about. The longer you are together alone, the lower your resistance.
2. Do not be in places where you could give too much away. Many people blew their commitment to keep sex special just because they put themselves in a position where it was hard to stop.

3. Fight wrong desires when they are only a thought. Guard what you watch, what you listen to, what you let your mind dwell on. If you let yourself think it, pretty soon you will want it, then do it, then pay for it.

4. Don't push to the point where your mind and body start preparing for intercourse. In other words, do not let yourself get into situations where you awaken desires you cannot satisfy righteously.

By taking practical actions such as these to defend the lines you have drawn around your love, you are reducing the pressure, respecting your Creator, and loving the person you will spend your life with. You are "avoiding" and "controlling" so you can be "reserved for something special."

Step 4: Declare a New Beginning

A future of love and sex at its best begins with a serious commitment to God about your body. I saw a young woman at a conference recently with a great shirt that simply said in bold letters, "Property of God." That's really who we are. First, your body is His handmade creation. Second, "Your body is a temple of the Holy Spirit.... You are not your own; you were bought at a price. Therefore honor God with your body" (1 Corinthians 6:19–20).

Because God made you, because God paid for you, and because God lives in you, it is only right that you give back to Him the body He gave you. Your body—all of it—is really the "property of God."

So, there is a commitment to your Creator that will launch you in a new beginning. Here it is:

"Lord, I promise You that I will keep my body pure, and I will keep sex special from now until my wedding night."

Would you be willing to make that pledge to God? You can be sure He will give you His supernatural strength to keep it, even when the pressure is on. This commitment marks for you a clear, bold first step on the road to sex at its best—sex God's way.

Many of you have already experienced sex at less than its best—*your* way. You may be feeling defensive, guilty, or shamed because of your past. And to you a new beginning seems impossible. But hear this: *Whatever you've done before today doesn't ever have to matter again.*

Many years ago, God communicated incredible good news to some people who had not kept sex special. He identifies some of the people He is talking about as the sexually immoral, adulterers, male prostitutes, homosexual offenders—all people who, maybe like you, had messed up in the sexual area of their lives. Here, then, is God's final word on people with a sexual past: "And that is what some of you were" (1 Corinthians 6:11).

Excuse me? Did God say *were*? How could that be?

"But you were *washed*, you were *sanctified*, you were *justified* in the name of the Lord Jesus Christ and by the Spirit of our God" (1 Corinthians 6:11).

Three amazing things had happened to these people. First, they had been washed—made clean! Secondly, they had been sanctified—no, not given robes and halos. Sanctified means "reserved for special purposes." These people had been "made special" again, especially when it came to the area of sex. And thirdly, they had been *jus-tified*—that means they were made okay with God again.

If it could happen to them, it could happen to you! But how can the guilt and scars of a sexual past be removed and healed like this? The answer is all wrapped up in these simple but powerful words—"In the name of the Lord Jesus Christ."

The hope of your new beginning is based totally on Jesus Christ. Why? Because, according to the Bible, "He himself bore our sins in his body on the tree, so that we might die to sins and live for righteousness" (1 Peter 2:24). That means God stands ready to erase every sin from His records in heaven, and you will never bear the guilt of them again. Just like when you take a shower after you've gotten really gross and dirty—you get washed, you get clean, and the dirt is gone!

What a Miracle!

Our daughter Lisa was in French class one day, and the teacher was late. So some of the girls started looking through the photos in each other's purses. Since Lisa was in her last year of high school, she had her senior picture with her. Long, naturally curly hair, big smile with those orthodontist-straight teeth, those big blue eyes—everybody thought she looked great!

Then she pulled out her picture from seventh grade. That was a very brave thing to do.

After all, not too many people go around showing folks what they looked like when they were twelve or thirteen. But Lisa laughed along with her friends at a much "geekier" Lisa—hair pulled back, braces from ear-to-ear, eyes partly hidden behind some distinctly *un*designer glasses. At that point, Madame French Teacher walked in. She took one look at the two faces of Lisa and pronounced a two-word verdict on what she saw—*"Quelle miracle!"* What a miracle!

Our daughter didn't care what people thought about the seventh-grade Lisa because of one simple fact. She could look at that picture and say, "That *was* me, but that's not me anymore!"

That is the miracle of being washed and forgiven by Jesus Christ. From the day you put your trust in Him to be your Savior, you can look back at all the sins of your past and say those liberating words—"That *was* me, but that's not me anymore!"

God is able to do what no therapist or counselor on earth could ever do. He can restore your spiritual and emotional virginity. He can "purify" you from the effects of your sexual mistakes. He can make sex *special* again for you. Only the Inventor of sex could do that. And He will start that healing process—the moment you claim His forgiveness and make Him the Lord of your body and your sexuality.

So, if you belong to this awesome Savior, whatever you've done before today doesn't ever have to matter again. And if you decide to let the Inventor of love be the Lord of your life, then He will give you what your heart really hopes for—sex at its best.

2 The Romance Rebels

Pursuing Dates Instead of Friends

Here's a little rhyming game. Think of words that rhyme with *dating*.

"Rating!" Good one. A lot of that is going on as guys look at girls and girls look at guys.

I can imagine a couple of guys standing on a street corner, checking out the girls. You can hear them mumbling their "ratings" to each other—six, four, three-and-a-half. Ah, but then two girls walk up to the great raters and announce that the girls have been watching them. "Really?" the guys reply excitedly—"How'd we do?" "Minus three!" And the two guys check themselves into the emergency room—for an ego transplant! Actually, dating and rating do go together a lot as everyone is checking out the prospects.

Of course, *baiting* rhymes with dating, too. And people are playing all kinds of games to attract and catch a girl or guy. Like a fisherman deciding which bait will attract the fish he wants, people fishing for a partner try to offer what their "fish" will go for.

Then there's *waiting*. That is what dating means to many people—waiting for something romantic to happen to them. There are probably more people waiting a lot than dating a lot!

There's another word that rhymes with dating—*hating*. The dating game can lead to you either hating someone you used to love—or hating yourself and asking questions like, "What's wrong with me?"

Actually, the way we date and rate people is not working very well, since half of the marriages our dating system produces break up! The system that is supposed to be producing love often gives us loneliness instead. Instead of bringing people closer together, it often leaves people farther apart.

But because romance is the only kind of male-female relationship most young people think about, that is the only kind they pursue. And pursuing a romance is pressure—pressure to impress him or her, get a relationship, keep a relationship, maintain a relationship, and define a relationship. "Are we just friends, brother and sister, seeing each other, going out, going steady, pre-engaged, engaged, committed, uncommitted, or confused?" Pressure!

The whole dating process is so superficial, so pressured, that it often leads to warped relationships. Let's look at three painful results of our current dating system.

The Lone Ranger

For starters, imagine a young woman who is dating one of those TV heroes of the Old West—the Lone Ranger. First of all, she is going to have to get used to having Tonto along as a chaperone all the time. The Lone Ranger's trusty Indian companion was his American Express card—he never left home without him! But even if this girl can get her man alone, she has a problem. It might surface like this:

Penelope: "Lone Ranger, I'm tired of calling you Lone Ranger. What's your name, big guy?"

Ranger: "Sorry, Penelope—my identity must remain a secret. But you may call me Ranger for short."

Penelope: "I can deal with that. But, well—you see ..."

Ranger: "What is it, Penelope? I want you to be honest with me."

Penelope: "Well, Ranger boy—it's ... it's the mask. "

Ranger: "What about it?"

Penelope: "I can't really get to know you if you insist on keeping that mask on! Something's got to change here!"

Ranger: "You're right, Penelope."

Penelope: "So you're taking off your mask?"

Ranger: "'Fraid not. Hi–ho, Silver!"

(*Sounds of hoofbeats fading into the distance*)

Penelope: (*spitting dust*) "Great. Well, who *was* that masked man?"

Tonto: "The Lone Ranger!"

Penelope: "Wait a minute. Who are you?"

Tonto: "Trusty Indian companion, Tonto. Wanna date?"

Penelope: "Never again."

What girl would want a relationship with the Lone Ranger if his identity was covered up with a mask? That is exactly what happens in many dating relationships. Many young people have gone out with someone who ended up being the Lone Ranger—or Rangerette. The pressure of dating creates an ugly result I call *masked strangers*.

Since impressing a guy or girl is critical to getting a guy or girl, most people wear a mask that will make an impression. Unfortunately, some people never find out who the real person was behind the mask—until it is too late. Many dating couples never really get to know each other as real people—they were too busy being lovers or impressers. And so many people have ended up looking at their husband or wife one day and realizing they married a stranger. Because getting and keeping a "date" is so often based on superficial attractions, many relationships never really get beyond the surface—even though they may get very involved physically.

Being "close" is what dating is supposed to be all about. Since a romantic relationship is often too pressurized for people to get emotionally real and emotionally close, they settle for getting physically close. And they end up with another ugly result of the pressure to be romantic: *love robbers*.

The Love Robber

You're together a lot, and it's just the two of you. You run out of things to talk about … you run out of things to do. Hello, making out. Hello, making big mistakes.

Yes, getting involved physically feels good. It can even feel like you are really getting close. But it can end up costing you love.

Anyone who has ever been involved in a physical relationship knows what happens—when you start touching, you stop talking! Sex is such a strong force that once it is unleashed in a relationship, it takes over. And much of the talking and communicating that really brings two people together—not just their bodies—is lost to the heat of making out. Honestly, it usually becomes, "How soon can we get to it?" And the "it" is not talking. So, the physical affection that was supposed to make you closer actually keeps you from really getting close.

In fact, because sexual love was designed by God to be expressed only inside a marriage relationship, it actually causes problems in a relationship that is not a marriage. If you are sexually active in a dating relationship, there is something in you, put there by the Inventor, that wants the deep commitment that is supposed to go with sex. So there starts to be jealous feelings of "owning" the other person, distrust—feelings that push people farther apart, not closer together.

And since you really only know each other's bodies, there is constant stress because you are still emotional strangers. Also, down deep inside there can be a loss of respect for the other person, a sense of guilt, and even resentment toward the one you are supposed to be getting closer to.

The Inventor of sex set the boundaries when He said, "You should avoid sexual immorality.... In this matter no one should wrong his brother or take advantage of him" (1 Thessalonians 4:3, 6). How does your physical relationship you are having with someone you are dating end up wronging someone else? By robbing your partner's future husband or wife of your partner's "unopened love gift." Plus everything you give someone other than your lifetime partner is something you are taking from your lifetime partner. In a sense, premarital sexual involvement is actually four-way robbery—stealing the uniqueness of married love from each other and from each other's future husband or wife.

Again, the pressures created by dating relationships tend to push you toward a physical relationship—and what that kind of relationship can cost you in real love.

The Strangler

Those "boyfriend/girlfriend" pressures can also produce another ugly result—*relationship stranglers.*

People can get "strangled" in a romance when it becomes too possessive. Once you have a dating relationship, you do not want to lose it—so some people hang on tight! Too tight! They act as if a relationship means ownership, holding a death grip on the other person as if their whole identity comes and goes with their partner. But that kind of "I own you now" approach ultimately does not preserve love, it crushes the life out of it. Unfortunately, the pressures of "having someone" tend to create a possessiveness that eventually drives people apart.

Girlaphobia

The call.

It can be one of the most terrifying experiences of male adolescence. You really want to go out with Jennifer. Friday night there's a show at school that would be a natural. You have the desire. You have the occasion. Now only one thing separates you from Jennifering. The call. You have to pick up that telephone and call the girl.

Practice. That's what you need. So you start rehears-
ing your "studly" approach. "Hello, Jennifer—this is Mike."
Deep voice—good! "I was hoping the most beautiful girl
in the school might be willing to go with me to the show
Friday night." Smooth—good! You're not fully satisfied
with your lines yet, so you keep polishing your pitch.
Forty-five minutes have now passed since you began this
rehearsal. You cannot put this off any longer.

With beads of sweat breaking out on your forehead,
you reach for the phone. You pull your hand back as if
high voltage was sizzling through that receiver. Cold feet.
But waiting is not going to make it any easier. So you
bravely pick up that receiver and punch in those seven
numbers that will bring you into Jennifer's presence. You
have practiced. You know what you are going to say.
Then suddenly, you hear that magic voice at the other
end—"Hi! This is Jennifer!"

Silence on your end. "Hello? Is anyone there?" the
sweet voice on her end asks. This is it. Taking a deep
breath, you give it everything you've got—"Hel-lo-oh."
No trace of that deep voice from rehearsal. All that comes
out is the squeaks you haven't heard since you were
twelve—and a "hello" delivered in three different octaves!

Once again, the pressure of the dating game has
melted another man to jello. And it is not just a male
thing. This strange couple thing we do makes both guys
and girls very tense about the impression they will make
and the response they will receive. It is pressure that produces another ugly result—*paralyzed prospects*.

The unnatural pressures of pairing up make just about
everyone tense and awkward. And because the risks of

rejection seem so strong, many people never ask or get asked. Which makes for a lot of frustrated, lonely people. And the lonely frustration is unnecessary! If we could just be friends, so much pressure could be avoided. But the rush to romance makes dating such a high-stakes risk that many quality people are left on the sidelines. Because all men and women do is date, many people who would make great coed friends sit paralyzed on the outside.

Perhaps the cruelest result of our "must date to rate" system is *defeated winners*.

A lot of winners are made to feel like losers in a system that only allows "boyfriends" and "girlfriends"—not boys who are friends and girls who are friends. Those who are not being "asked out" keep asking that haunting question, "What's wrong with me?" The answer probably is, "Nothing." But it sure doesn't feel that way. Many solid-gold guys and girls get passed over in the cruel narrowness of the dating game.

God makes it clear that He only created winners when He says, "We are God's workmanship, created in Christ Jesus to do good works, which God prepared in advance for us to do" (Ephesians 2:10). You may not be dated, rated, or appreciated—but nothing can change the fact that you are a masterpiece workmanship of our Creator. You have incalculable worth and incredible work to do on this planet. No boyfriend or girlfriend can make you worth any more. God is the One who gave you your value—not someone who happens to ask you out. But because of the pressures of a system that says "No guy, no good" or "No girl, no good," a lot of masterpieces feel like junk.

There is nothing wrong with you. There is something wrong with the system that makes you believe that lie.

Just Friends?

"Just friends" sounds like a real bummer to most young people—especially in an upside-down culture that keeps telling you that being someone's "boyfriend" or "girlfriend" is all that counts. But the Romance Rebels don't believe that lie. They know that "Friends" is first prize in guy-girl relationships, not the consolation prize!

The way to a great romance is not by trying to have a great romance. It's by having great friendships. The greatest romances in the world began as great friendships! So your goal for your relationships with the opposite sex is to have as many friends as you can. Someday one of those friendships may grow naturally into a romance—but one that is a love relationship between friends, not strangers!

The Bonuses of Friendship

Romance Rebels have decided to challenge the dating system that keeps us apart and go for the "something better" of coed friendships. Why? Because they have seen that the pressures of the dating game just aren't worth it … and the payoffs of building friendships really are worthwhile. Let's look at some.

You Can Develop the Real You

When you are trying to play the "must impress" games of dating, you tend to wear whatever mask will do the job. But part of the payoff of coed friendships is that you can develop the real you, without any mask. Being real is actually the starting point for authentic love. In God's words, "Love must be sincere" (Romans 12:9).

That is the beauty of being friends with the opposite sex. You can relax ... be yourself ... enjoy each other without so much of the tension of impressing or getting involved in the "how far are we going to go?" games.

Ultimately, you are going to want to spend your life with someone who appreciates the real you, not the masked you. Those kinds of relationships have a chance to develop in the garden of coed friendship.

You Can Develop Where You Are Weak

Another payoff of coed friendships is that you can develop where you are weak.

Once when my son Brad was with me and some friends in a restaurant, I noticed he kept trying to get my attention without attracting everyone else's. He was pointing to his upper lip. I thought maybe he wanted me to pass the lip balm or something. Finally, I realized what the "charades" had been about. He informed me quietly that I was carrying some remains of my dinner on my upper lip—and probably grossing out the rest of the table. I leaned over to him and said, "Thanks—but I'm actually saving it for later. I might want a snack." He rolled his eyes as if to say, "Why do I even bother?"

Frankly, I'm glad he does. We all need someone who will care enough to tell us the things that need some attention. In a way, Brad was being my mirror. Friends can do that for each other.

This is not exactly a news flash, but men and women do see the world a little differently. That's one of the reasons you need friendships with the opposite sex. A girl can see some of a guy's weak spots that another guy might never see. And a guy can see some of a girl's "need to work on" areas that another girl might never see.

If you are a guy, a girl who is a friend might help you grow by pointing out things such as these:

"Girls respond best to guys who don't talk about themselves most of the time."

"I like it when you do the gentleman thing. Do it more."

"Don't be afraid to show your feelings—it makes people want to be around you."

If you are a girl, a guy who is a friend might help you grow with observations such as these:

"Don't just shut down when you're hurt—work through it!"

"Give guys a chance to get their feelings out—we need a lot of encouragement."

"When you worry like that, it doesn't change anything. Let it go."

Those are only examples of how friends of the opposite sex can be two-legged mirrors to help you see what needs improving. It isn't always pleasant to hear that we "have part of our dinner on our face," but it is worse to never be told. And because coed friendships are not the high-pressure, high-stakes kind of relationships that romances are, we are more willing to be honest with each other—and to take someone's encouragement to change. As the Bible says, "As iron sharpens iron, so one man sharpens another" (Proverbs 27:17).

That "sharpening" can happen in a beautiful way as coed friends help each other develop the areas that need

work. In a dating relationship, we often try to cover up
our own weaknesses, and we are afraid to confront the
other person's. In a friendship, we tend to be more open
... and we can really help each other become all we were
meant to be.

You Can Develop Your Confidence

Another payoff of building friendships with the
opposite sex is you can develop your confidence. This is
what the Bible means when it says to tell each other
"what is helpful for building others up according to their
needs" (Ephesians 4:29).

God wants us to be looking for the strong points in
other people—strengths we can affirm and encourage in
them. And it is a special gift of encouragement when it
comes from a guy to a girl or a girl to a guy. When you
are dating, your mirror inputs are limited. When you are
developing many friends of the opposite sex, you have
many mirrors.

You Can Develop Your Friendship Skills

For many guys, knowing how to relate to girls does
not come naturally. It's the same for girls with guys. And
a dating relationship is a high-pressure environment in
which to learn! On the other hand, friendship provides a
more relaxed setting where we can come with all our
insecurities and practice relating in a lower-risk situation.

As you spend time with friends of the opposite sex,
you can learn how to talk with them, listen to them,
understand them, have fun with them, pray with them,
encourage them, confront them. One day you may meet

the person who may be your ultimate friend on earth, the person you might marry. And you will know how to treat and love that person because of all you learned in the "dress rehearsal" of your coed friendships.

The Ultimate Matchmaker

I will never forget that day.

The baby girl I held in my hands for 2:00 A.M. feedings not long ago was now the radiant young woman in the bridal gown, waiting to march down the aisle. A thousand thoughts and feelings flooded over me as she took my arm and I escorted her down that aisle to the man she loved. It was a tender day for me, but not a sad one. The man I would give Lisa to was a man I totally loved and respected.

At that emotional moment when Lisa left my arm and took the arm of her groom, I spoke to Rick, welcoming him to our family. But the great joy of that moment was to be able to say, "Rick, you are the man we have prayed for since Lisa was born ... we have prayed for a man who was prepared, chosen, and kept by God for Lisa, and you are the answer to our prayers."

We had been talking to the greatest Matchmaker in the universe for over twenty years about His perfect partner for our daughter—and God did it again as He has done millions of times over thousands of years.

He wants to do that for you—if you will let Him find you a mate instead of you finding one for yourself. You build healthy coed friendships ... let God make one into the ultimate romance. You do not have to join all the "hunting parties" out there, chasing a girl or a guy. God has someone very special for you, and you can be talking to Him about that person every day. In the meantime, enjoy the trip and prepare for your destination by developing a network of great male-female friendships.

There is a biblical prayer that should probably be on a plaque in the room of every young person who wants the very best in lifetime love. "Let her [or him] be the one the LORD has chosen" (Genesis 24:44). If that is your prayer, you can relax, knowing that you do not have to play romantic Russian roulette in the "must have a boyfriend" or "must have a girlfriend" sweepstakes. You can focus on quality friendships with the confidence that the Ultimate Matchmaker will one day lead you to your God-prepared, God-sent partner. And if God's plan for you is to be more fulfilled and more effective without a husband or wife, you will always be rich in male and female friendships because you have given your love needs to Him.

You can be so free and secure emotionally if you choose to let your loving heavenly Father meet your deepest emotional needs rather than you running around trying to get them met. When it comes to your relationships and your romance, the directions and promises of Psalm 37 can make all the difference— "Delight yourself in the LORD, and he will give you the desires of your heart. Commit your way to the LORD; trust in him and he will do this" (vv. 4–5).

The "Is This Really Love?" Test

I was probably "in love" a dozen times in my first eighteen years—starting with a redhead named Helen in fifth grade. Each time after that it was a little more like the real thing, but none of those were real love—the lifetime kind.

But I often wondered how I could tell if "this is really love." We know we want real love, but what is it? After watching probably thousands of couples over some thirty years, I have begun to define "real love." I ask twelve questions in my "Is This Really Love?" test.

1. Do I usually put their needs first?

Real love is summed up in three words—"Put them first." Love takes you beyond your natural focus on yourself and makes you want to focus on the other person's needs and welfare. God shows us the word that proves it is love when He tells us to "live a life of love, just as Christ loved us and gave himself up for us as a ... sacrifice to God" (Ephesians 5:2). Sacrifice. That is what love makes a person do. Like Jesus, you are willing to give up yourself for the sake of someone you truly love.

2. Can we take off all our masks with each other?

Authentic love moves past the superficiality of two people impressing each other to the reality of two people being themselves with each other. There is a "nothing to prove, nothing to hide" quality to lifetime love. You are able to speak "the truth in love" (Ephesians 4:15) to each other. When you really love someone, you feel safe enough to trust the real you—warts and all—to that person.

3. Would we still love each other if we didn't touch each other?

Passion can blind you with feelings that mimic love but are not love. When a relationship gets heavily physical, it becomes harder to know if what you are feeling is really love. A lot of people have made a lifetime love mistake because their glands deceived them into thinking this was the right person. If you want to be able to make a "no regrets" choice about love, it is wise to develop your relationship with this advice God gave to young men about their male-female relationships—"Treat ... [the] younger women as sisters, with absolute purity" (1 Timothy 5:2).

4. Do we handle conflict without really hurting each other?

Your disagreeing times are an important test of whether this is a lifetime love. How do you handle the issues and incidents that could tear you apart and leave painful scars? God's way is to "not let the sun go down while you are still angry" (Ephesians 4:26) and to "bear with each other and forgive whatever grievances you may have against one another" (Colossians 3:13). Authentic love does not demand its own way ... it fixes things quickly ... it does not scar the other person ... it does not hold grudges.

5. Has this relationship stood the test of lots of real-life experiences?

The test of love is time—time to have more than romantic dates. Marriage is not just one date after another—it is going through paying bills together, having the flu, deciding how to manage your money, being with each other when you are really tired or grumpy, dealing with each other's parents together, and so on. Before you decide you will be with a person for life, you need to know what he or she is like in a lot of life experiences and pressures. And that takes time. Without knowing a person, there is no loving a person; without time with a person, there is no knowing that person. Only extended time together will show if this is solid-gold love—the kind that "always protects, always trusts, always hopes, always perseveres" (1 Corinthians 13:7). In the words of a popular song of the sixties, "You can't hurry love."

6. Do we consistently have intelligent things to talk about?

When you are talking about a lifetime with someone, you want to be sure you will never get bored with your partner. One good way to test that is with this question. Are you able to have consistently interesting conversations with this person you love? You want to marry someone who you will never get tired of, not someone who is like a shallow well where you quickly run out of water.

7. Are you proud of the way they act in public?

You will want to spend your life with someone who treats you and others with respect in public situations.

8. Are you proud of the way they act in private?

Some people look great when people are around but are very different when you are with them alone. It does not matter how proud you may be of the one you love in public if they do not treat you right in private. How your partner treats you when no one is looking tells you a lot about the depth of their love for you.

9. Can I accept constructive criticism from them?

You might look pretty scary if you never looked in a mirror. We need mirrors to tell us that another oil well has erupted on our face, that our hair exploded, that we are unzipped. Mirrors do not always give us good news, but they give us news we need. Even more than glass mirrors, we need human mirrors—people who love us enough to tell us what we need to work on. Your lifetime partner ought to be your #1 mirror. You need to be able to accept the constructive criticism that comes from the person who loves you most—without reacting as if you are under attack.

10. Do I know their weaknesses and can I live with them?

Young love tends to minimize a lover's weaknesses and maximize a lover's strengths. For example, a young woman might describe her boyfriend like this: "Oh, he's handsome and considerate and generous—oh, he's a teeny disorganized—but he's so handsome, so considerate." That's before she is married to him. After you are married, suddenly those weaknesses that you minimized before start to look huge. "Oh sure, he looks good and he's generous sometimes—but he is so disorganized, he drives me nuts!" Before you make a lifetime commitment, make sure you can live with this person's weak points for a lifetime. "Oh, I'll change him," you say—don't count on it. Many people were counting on a fairy-tale ending where their kisses would miraculously turn a frog into a prince—and ended up with a frog for fifty years! Assume that those weaknesses will never change. The choice to marry a person is a choice to live with their weak points as well as their strengths.

11. Do I love them even when they are at their worst?

The ultimate test of the depth of your love is how you respond when that person is the least lovable. If you cannot love your partner when he or she is unlovable, this is probably not a love that will last. "A friend loves at all times, and a brother is born for adversity" (Proverbs 17:17).

12. Is it natural for us to talk about Jesus and talk to Jesus together?

The strongest love relationships in the world are those with Jesus Christ in the center. He is the glue when not much else is holding you together. He is the place to go for unconditional love when your love has run out. He is the place you can meet when you cannot agree on anything else. He is your harbor when the storms are really intense around you. Jesus promised that "where two or three come together in my name, there am I with them" (Matthew 18:20). What an awesome promise to a couple in love! The question is do you often "come together in His name"? If it is unnatural for the two of you to talk about Him and talk to Him together, then how can He ever be the center of your relationship? If you have a personal relationship with Jesus Christ and the person you marry does not care much about Him, you will be emotionally torn in two your whole life. No earth-love is worth sacrificing Jesus for. If you both share an eternal bond with Jesus Christ, you can experience a bond and an intimacy together that those without Jesus will never know.

Yes, the old saying tells us that "love is blind." Actually, real love has its eyes wide open. It is a deep, unselfish commitment that has counted the cost, asked the hard questions, and decided to live sacrificially for the other person's welfare. This is love that you can build a life on.

3 The Play-Doh Squeeze

TICKING TIME BOMB #3:
Letting Your Friends Decide Who You Are

The Christmas season may be fun for kids, but it can be combat for mommies and daddies. Combat, as in fighting a zillion other parents to find the "super-toy" of the season. I'm convinced there must be a toy guru somewhere who decides what those toys will be this year. Their goal? Get the "Intergalactic Destructo-Ranger" on every kid's Christmas list so every parent who doesn't buy one feels like a total failure.

Over the years, I have watched a lot of "toy of the year" selections hit high tide, then recede. Depending on the ages of our children, we parents have chased Star Wars figures, Cabbage Patch dolls, Power Rangers, Tickle-Me Elmos, Nintendo 64—whatever those TV commercials made a generation drool over.

But as the toy fads have come and gone, there is one plaything that has stood the test of time. It is not very sophisticated, not very slick. It doesn't have joysticks, batteries, or wardrobes for every occasion—but it has been a must for the children of several generations. This long-lasting entertainer comes in those little round, plastic containers with different-colored lids. Inside is this soft, inviting substance that matches the color of the lid. Yes! What else could it be but the reigning champion of decades of Toy Wars—Play-Doh!

That soft, colorful clay has been molded by many a young sculptor—and found all through carpets in millions of homes. Let's face it—Play-Doh is fun! Of course, it comes out in the shape of the can … but then you can make it into any shape you want—flat like a pancake, long like a hot dog, round like a ball, in one piece or several pieces. Doesn't just the thought of all those creative possibilities make you want to go to the shelf right now and open a can of the magic clay?

A Play-Doh toy is great.

A Play-Doh person is not.

Play-Doh People

All day long, the people around you are trying to squeeze you into the shape they want you to be. If they succeed, you will be another Play-Doh person. And you will be in the danger zone where a time bomb is ticking that could devastate your future—letting your friends decide who you are.

When that happens, your identity becomes like a constantly reshaped blob of Play-Doh. When you're with your party friends, they squeeze you until you look like them. When you're with your parents, you become the shape that will keep them happy. When you're with church people, church shape … with "tough" friends, "tough" shape … "cool" friends, "cool" shape … whatever shape the "squeezers" like, a Play-Doh person will conform to it. Which means you have little or no identity of your own. You become like one young woman who told me, "I have so many masks for so many different people—I don't even know who I am anymore!"

It's sad when there are so many different "you's" that you lose track of who "you" are! But the pressure is heavy to do whatever will keep you from being rejected or ridiculed by people you have to see all the time. And when you don't dance to their tune, they pull out one or more of the "Classic Lines for Getting People to Do the Wrong Thing."

- "Everybody's doing it!"
- "A little won't hurt."
- "No one will ever know."
- "You chicken?"
- "It's fun, man!"
- "If you love me, you will ..."
- "Just this once ..."
- "If it feels good, do it!"

Ultimately, there are two words that sum up the choices of a Play-Doh person: *Fit in!*

That's the drumbeat of the people around you— "Wear what we wear, talk like we talk, listen to what we listen to. Call cool what we call cool, laugh at what we laugh at, go where we go, do what we do." Fit in! When you're young and not real sure of who you really are just yet, you do not want to be the outsider or the one who sticks out. So the slave masters of peer pressure just keep chanting in your heart, "Fit in. Fit in. Fit in."

However the pressure comes, it never advertises the price tag for giving in. Just ask the people who made one compromise, which made the next compromise easier, which led to lots of compromises—which ultimately cost them treasures such as their virginity, their reputation, their freedom, their parents' trust, their closeness to God.

Most of us are puppets in the hands of the people we want to please—who are puppets in the hands of the people they want to please, and so on. So, we walk around to each person or group of people, holding out our "Am I okay?" ticket, hoping they will stamp it with their approval. In fact, most of us are approval junkies, trying to get as many "You're okay's" as we can. Problem: Approval junkies always need another fix!

If five people give you the "thumbs up," there is always a sixth person whose okay you need, and a tenth, and a hundredth. There is never enough approval—so you have to keep performing for each group you are with—and each group has a shape they want you to be in order to get their "stamp." Hello, Play-Doh! Once you make approval your deciding factor, then you have to make "fitting in" your lifestyle. And since there is never enough approval, you have to play a lot of different "fit in" games, and each time give up another piece of you.

Better Than Play-Doh

If you're tired of being a Play-Doh person—or you're determined you don't want to become one—then consider the better idea: be a rock!

If you are the scientific type, just go outside and pick up a rock. Squeeze it until the veins stick out in your forehead. It won't change shape. If you want to take the experiment to another level, give that rock to Arnold Schwarzenegger—see how he does squeezing it. It won't change shape, no matter how heavy the pressure.

This could be you: a person so solid all the way through that you will not change shape, no matter who tries to squeeze you into their shape. When you are a rock person, there is only one you! There is no longer a closetful of you's for each occasion. You finally know who you are—and stay who you are no matter where you are.

It is the kind of gutsy, "no regrets" living you get when you step up to a Designer lifestyle. In the words of the Designer, "Don't copy the behavior and customs of this world, but let God transform you into a new person by changing the way you think. Then you will know what God wants you to do, and you will know how good and pleasing and perfect his will really is" (Romans 12:1–2 NLT).

"Conformed" means who you are and how you act is determined by what—or who—is outside you. God shows us something far better, far more secure. "Let God transform you." That means who you are and how you act is determined by what—or who—is on the inside. One of the most exciting benefits of having a personal relationship with God is that you have from Him this perfect inner guidance system. Just as the internal guidance system of a missile directs it to the right target, God directs His children to what He made them to do.

God's map is in the Bible, the only book He ever wrote. Once you find out God's viewpoint on an issue and commit yourself to live by it, you are ready to say,

"Good-bye, Play-Doh ... hello, rock!" You are no longer blown around by the shifting winds of what your friends want you to do—you are directed from the inside through God and His Word. When you base your life on the never-changing, always-right principles of God's own words, you move beyond being a blob of clay, constantly squeezed into whatever shape people want you to be in.

Now you have something stronger inside than the peer pressure outside. For example, the Play-Doh person says, "You haven't had sex yet? Do it, man—what are you waiting for?"

The Rock person answers, "Marriage should be honored by all, and the marriage bed kept pure.... It is God's will ... that you should avoid sexual immorality" (Hebrews 13:4; 1 Thessalonians 4:3).

The Play-Doh person calls, "Come on and have a drink with us—have a good time!"

The Rock person answers, "Wine is a mocker and beer a brawler; whoever is led astray by them is not wise" (Proverbs 20:1; see 31:4).

"Who cares what your parents say?" the Play-Doh person scoffs.

But the Rock person replies, "Honor your father and mother ... that it may go well with you and that you may enjoy long life on the earth" (Ephesians 6:2–3).

"Just a little won't hurt ... just this one time ..." says the Play-Doh person.

But the Rock knows better. "Have nothing to do with the fruitless deeds of darkness, but rather expose them. For it is shameful even to mention what the disobedient do in secret" (Ephesians 5:11–12).

When you have this kind of inner guidance from your Creator, you can be the mold instead of being the Play-Doh. You can lead instead of follow. Instead of letting your friends decide who you are, you are now living in the safety of letting your Creator decide who you are. You have put the mushy "Play-Doh you" back in the can once and for all and traded it in for a solid "rock you."

A Faceful of Pie, an Armful of Garbage

Sometimes in high school assemblies, I have called five students up to the stage to play "The Persuaders Game." Four of them form a square around a fifth student who stands in the middle of them, blindfolded. Then the four corner people are each given something to hold in their hands. One has a ten-dollar bill—that's the good news. The other three are holding a whipped cream pie, a bag of garbage, and a super-soaker squirt gun, respectively. At the signal, each corner person has ten seconds to persuade Mr. Blindfold to come to his or her corner. Needless to say, three of them just lie, telling their friend that "I have the ten dollars—come to me!" And, of course, one is telling the truth about having the cash. Finally, I ask Mr. Blindfold to go to one of those corners and "your friend will give you whatever he or she has." As he is trying to decide who to trust, all four of his friends are yelling at him, trying to persuade him to come and get what they have. Why? Because if any of the "persuaders" who does not have the money lures him to their corner, that persuader gets the money! It's not good to reward lying like that, but the whole experiment makes an important point.

Sometimes Mr. Blindfold follows a voice and ends up with good stuff. But, unfortunately, his odds are three to one that he will end up either with a faceful of pie, an armful of garbage, or a drenching. No matter how it turns out, that game offers a picture of most young people every day of their lives. There are many voices, all trying to pull you in their direction—and most of them will mess you up if you go their way. But in the din of "do this!" and "try this!" voices around you, there is one Voice you can trust—One who will lead you only to the good stuff.

MADmen! MADwomen!

Getting our kids—Lisa, Doug, and Brad—off to school each morning was always quite an adventure—finding socks, books, homework, and car keys. After that family circus, the three junior Hutchcrafts marched out the back door to meet their academic destiny. As they started across the yard, I would yell two words of profound parental wisdom: "Go MAD!"

"What kind of irresponsible father are you," you may ask, "telling your children to be insane in school today?" But my children knew what that meant. "Go MAD" means "Go Make A Difference!" As I told my kids, "You are not on this planet primarily to make money, make grades, make a team, or make an impression—you are here to make a difference."

In fact, your Creator says, "We are God's workmanship, created in Christ Jesus to do good works, which God prepared in advance for us to do" (Ephesians 2:10). He did not put us here to "fit in" or "sit around," but to make a difference. When you think like a "MADman" or "MAD-woman," you make up your mind to shape other people, not have other people shape you, to change your environment instead of letting your environment change you. You stop playing defense, just fighting to keep your faith alive—and you start playing offense, working to live your faith in front of your friends.

And one rousing five-letter word becomes your order from the One who made you to make a difference. That word is *stand*. "Put on the full armor of God so that you can take your *stand* against the devil's schemes.... So that when the day of evil comes, you may be able to *stand* your ground, and after you have done everything, to *stand*. *Stand* firm then" (Ephesians 6:11, 13, 14).

Stand. Hold your ground. Don't retreat. *Stand* is the opposite of "go with the flow, do what everybody's doing, fit in." You decide where your boundaries are, what you will never do, what kind of person you will always be—and you go out each day to *stand!*

When you take a stand for what is right or against what is wrong, you can expect some interesting responses.

People Will Test You

Once you take a stand, people will put on some extra pressure to see if they can still shape the Play-Doh. Your response? "If sinners entice you, do not give in to them" (Proverbs 1:10).

People Will Begin to Accept You

The payoff for passing the temptation test a few times is that the people who are really your friends will simply accept these new convictions or boundaries as being part of who you are. Many of them will lighten up on the pressure, knowing you are going to "stand." And if you lose any friends because you stand for what is right, it was not friends you lost. Maybe acquaintances or party people, but not friends. Taking a stand does not usually cost you friends; it reveals who your friends really are.

People Will Come to Respect You

Many people wish they had the courage or strength to say no to some choices they know are hurting them and hurting others. They will actually—and probably quietly—wish they could be like you. God's promise to God-pleasers is that "when a man's ways are pleasing to the LORD, he makes even his enemies live at peace with him" (Proverbs 16:7).

People Will Begin to Defend You

Finally, don't be surprised if some people even get to the place where they defend you and the stand you are taking. I saw this happen again and again in our daughter Lisa's life. When she was in high school, she was very popular and active. Her friends, like most of the students in our school, were party people—but they knew Lisa had a "rock" stand against drinking, sex before marriage, and profanity. It never seemed to cost her friends. They wanted her around and seemed to respect the stand she took. And when people would ask her friends about getting Lisa to do some things she was against, it was her friends—who were partyers themselves—who defended her and said, "Leave her alone. She doesn't do that!"

I often wondered how Lisa could be so strong against certain behaviors and yet so well liked by people who did those things. The answer was that this same young woman who had strong convictions showed strong caring for her friends. She was the one who did special remembrances for their birthdays, who cared when they missed school, who always had a word of encouragement for them.

This attractive mixture of convictions and caring came together at a birthday party one night. Lisa knew the parents would be home, so she went. Well, evidently someone was supplying drinks in the bushes behind the house. Lisa's friend Amy (name changed) had a lot to drink early in the evening—and was kneeling by a bush, throwing up violently. All of Amy's drinking friends left her there in her misery. Lisa heard about Amy's situation and went out to be with her—holding Amy's hair as she continued to vomit. Lisa had often taken her stand against drinking—that was her well-known conviction. But that night she reached out with caring to a friend who was a victim of her own bad choices. One little post-script: as Amy was on her last "upheaval," Lisa did ask her one gutsy question—"Amy, is this one of those 'good times' you keep telling me you have when you drink?" She had more than won the right to ask that question!

Your friends, your school are in desperate need of a "Make A Difference" person—someone who really believes in something.

How to Turn Play-Doh into Rock

Most of us start out as Play-Doh, easily molded by the people around us. But some get tired of being every sculptor's slave and decide to become a "Make A Difference" person. If you're at that point, then you are ready for that scientifically amazing feat—changing mushy Play-Doh into solid rock. The formula has four steps.

Step 1: Choose Your Uniform

"I'm tired of gettin' shot at," says the Civil War soldier. So, he comes up with what he considers a brilliant idea. "I'm goin' to wear a blue coat and gray pants—that way I can make everybody happy." Bad idea. Instead, he ends up getting shot at on both ends! Why? Because he did not pick his side and choose his uniform. As long as you keep trying to wear more than one uniform in order to please different sides, you're going to get shot at on both ends. If you want to reduce the pressure on you, decide which you you're going to be and be that person all the time. When you keep flip-flopping back and forth, everyone thinks you are still going to go their way—so they keep pressuring you. When you choose your uniform once and for all, people will finally quit trying to get you to desert to the other side—and the pressure will decrease. Inconsistency increases peer pressure.

Step 2: Trade in "Clothes" for "Skin"

A doctor friend of ours was amazed when his teenage son asked if he could borrow a sport coat and pants of his to wear to school. Dad was really flattered—until his son told him why. "Oh, it's Geek Day at school, Dad." Actually, most young people are not very interested in wearing their parents' clothes—the clothes probably would not even fit. Young people cannot wear their parents' beliefs either—or their church's or their youth leader's—they need their own. The difference between firsthand and secondhand beliefs is like the difference between skin and clothes. You change your clothes for different occasions—work, school, the beach, dressy dates, bumming at home. But you always have the same skin!

Maybe the reason you have kept changing who you are for different people is because your beliefs are just clothes—and you change them for different occasions. Your Play-Doh will not turn to rock until you get with God and settle "What do I really believe?" about the major issues in your life. When it's between you and God, then it's skin—and you never change your skin, no matter what the occasion.

Step 3: Travel with People Who Are Going Where You Are Going

Sometimes you see hitchhikers beside the road, holding some crudely made sign with the name of some state or city on it—like "Milwaukee," let's say. This pilgrim is not especially interested in your SAT scores, your personality, or even what kind of chariot you have—he just wants to hook up with someone who is going where he wants to go. That's how you ought to pick your friends. First, of course, you have to decide what kind of person you want to become, what kind of goals you want to achieve. Then you need to look for people who have the same "destination sign" out as you do. Your selection of friends may well be *the* most important choice you will make as a young person—because you will probably end up on the same road as they do. That is why the Bible warns us that "bad company corrupts good character"

(1 Corinthians 15:33) and that "he who walks with the wise grows wise, but a companion of fools suffers harm" (Proverbs 13:20).

Step 4: Tie Every No to a Yes

There's an old song where a mountain-type guy brags, "I don't smoke, and I don't chew, and I don't go with the girls who do!" That's nice—we know what he's against ... now what is he *for*? Being a "MAD" person does not mean you are known only for the things you don't believe in and won't do. Every action you are against is because of something valuable that you are for. We are against choices that will ruin the most valuable treasures in life. So, a "Make A Difference" person is mostly a positive person, committed to protect some very positive possessions.

Seven Positive Ways to Say No

"Well, why can't you do it?" "Why" is what people want to know when you say no to some action or activity. And often that is where our eyes start darting back and forth and our mind races for a reason. Sometimes, the lack of a good reason makes us actually back down on our no.

When you have to take your stand, here are seven positive ways to say no.

1. "I want to stay in mint condition."

Any baseball card collector understands that a card is most valuable if it has no creases, no rounded corners, no "dings"—in other words, if it is in mint condition. That is also true of your body, your mind, your reputation, and your future—you have to keep them in mint condition if you want to preserve their value. And that is a very positive reason for saying no to something that could damage your value.

2. "My motto is 'No regrets.'"

That is a very positive way to explain why you are avoiding a choice that could leave you with later regrets or scars. You want to go to sleep at night guilt-free and regret-free.

3. "The Inventor knows best."

Since God invented us, He knows how we run best—and what will hurt us. Your personal boundaries are based not on where your church or parents draw the line, but on where your Creator does.

4. "My 'Coach' doesn't want me to."

If you want an Olympic future, you stay inside your coach's training rules. If Jesus Christ is your life-Coach, then you do what your Coach says is best.

5. "No viruses in my computer."

In God's own words, "Above all else, guard your heart, for it is the wellspring of life" (Proverbs 4:23). So why do you decide not to watch or listen to certain things? Because you are trying to protect the "computer" of your mind from any "viruses" that could mess up your program.

6. "The tape is always running."

God's tape, that is. The Bible assures us that "a man's ways are in full view of the LORD, and he examines all his paths" (Proverbs 5:21). Not only is God recording every input and every activity, so are your mind and body and soul. Today's choices are tomorrow's memories, and tomorrow's judgment.

7. "It would hurt Someone who loves me a lot."

The "Someone" is none other than Jesus Christ—the One who died on the cross "so that we might die to sins" (1 Peter 2:24). When you do the things that He had to die for, it really hurts Him. Ultimately, your choices are based on not doing what will hurt the One who loves you most. Not because of your religion or some rule book. It's because of your most important relationship! This is the most positive reason in the world for saying no. Living for Jesus Christ is about love, not laws. You do the things that make Him happy; you say no to the things that make Him sad.

It's time to turn in your Play-Doh. Not the kind you play with. The kind you've been too often. For long enough, the people around you have squeezed you into the shapes they wanted. It's time you stepped up to being who you were born to be: someone who can make a difference.

4 Mission Home Improvement

Forty thousand dollars for a summer job?

For real. Two teenagers from New England—a brother and sister—recently pulled in forty grand from their summer job! That sure beats slinging French fries at a fast-food place!

Actually, it was their father's idea. It began when he offered to teach his son and daughter how to build a house. Now, this probably didn't sound like Dream Summer to them—until Dad said the two of them could split the profit on the sale of the home they built! Needless to say, they signed up for a hammer and saw immediately.

Those two teenagers worked long and hard—laying the foundation, building the walls, installing the plumbing, wiring the electricity. By the end of the summer, they hammered their last boards—to make a "For Sale" sign to put in the front yard. And the best trip they took that summer was to the bank—with their sale profit of $40,000. What a head start on college!

Two young people learned to build a home—and it really paid off!

Actually, few things could pay off more for you than doing some home-building of your own. No, not the kind of building where you wear a nail apron and annoy your neighbors wailing with a power saw all day. The home construction project you may need to tackle is building or rebuilding your family. And the payoff isn't the kind you take to the bank—it's the kind that pays off with a future of relationships that deliver love, not hurt.

Of course, a lot of young people have never thought about trying to change their family—they're just trying to *survive* their family. After all, your mother is always going to be—well, the mother she's always been, right? Same for your father, your brother, your sister. It's easy to assume your relationships with them—the good stuff, the bad stuff, the ugly stuff—are just always going to be that way and to leave your years at home with wounds inside that even seventy years may not heal.

Often, it isn't until years later that you realize how long family pain can last—and how it can affect your own marriage, your own kids, your own future happiness. Like most of our life-scarring "time bombs," we often don't realize until later how much damage it will do—or how far the damage will reach. We can defuse the explosion, though, if we confront the mistake that will blow up your future happiness.

"Surviving" Your Family Instead of Improving Your Family

There is no family quite like yours—and whatever it's like, it doesn't have to stay the way it is—if some family member would step up and say, "I want to make a difference!"

You may be in a single-parent family, a two-parent family (if you have an older sister, you may have a two-mother family!), or a blended family. "Home" for you may be a happy word or a hurting word—or maybe both. You may have a cuddly "teddy bear family" or one where everyone is just a bear. It could be a silent place where nobody talks, a communicative place where everybody talks, or a war zone place where everybody talks loud and mean. Whatever the situation, there is a lot about your family that you did not choose, that you have no control over.

Still, you can make a difference there, no matter how happy or unhappy things are at home. But before you'll use the "how to" of improving your family relationships, you have to have a "want to."

Bad News on the Thermometer

My nose was the first to get the message when I woke up one winter morning—it felt like Lassie's nose. It was cold! But, then, so was our whole house! My next clue that something was wrong was the first contact my feet had with uncarpeted floor. I invented a new dance right there. When I checked the thermometer, it told me what my body already knew—it was only forty degrees in our house! I was tempted to go outside to get warm! I went away muttering as I headed for the kitchen to turn on the oven.

Later, the kids wandered into the kitchen one at a time, only to find me having my morning prayer time in front of an open oven. Since my eyes were closed, my wife told me how each child reacted. Brad, about four at the time, walked around my chair, looking at me quizzically. Then six-year-old Doug strolled in, took one look, and asked, "Mommy, why is Daddy praying to the stove?" Eight-year-old Lisa just blurted, "Oh, great stove, please keep us warm!"

Actually, the solution for our personal North Pole was a simple phone call to Mr. Heating Company. His inspection revealed that our problem was not, of course, the thermometer—it was the thermostat! That temperature-controlling device was not working, so the temperature at our house was not very livable.

There is a big difference between a thermometer and a thermostat. A thermometer reflects the temperature; a thermostat sets the temperature. So, which one are you in your family?

Do you just see how they treat you and then treat them the same way? Hello, thermometer! "If you're hot, then I'm hot! If you're cold, then I'm cool! If you're nice, I'm nice. If you share, I'll share. If you listen, I'll listen. If you yell, I'll yell." If you live like that most of the time, you are a thermometer, just reflecting the temperature everyone else sets.

But you can be a thermostat! You can help set the temperature at your house. In other words, you decide how you would like things to be, and you start acting that way yourself.

When a young person decides to be a thermostat rather than a thermometer at home, he or she becomes the hope of something better in that family. That means moving beyond the fatalistic mind-set of just "surviving" your family to the hope-giving mission of improving your family. And there may be no mission on earth more important to your future and to your personal happiness.

Why? Because you will carry your family relationships around inside you wherever you go for the rest of your life! A teenage friend of mine once told me, "My problems are almost over. I'll be eighteen in a few months, and I will finally be out of my family!" I said, "You'll be out of your family, but how are you going to get your family out of you?"

The truth is, you never really do. Every adult has found that out—but usually too late ... long after the years when they could have tried to make a difference. But you are still in those years. That is why it is so important that you decide right now that you are going to try to set a better temperature in your family relationships. You want to leave home with those relationships in the best shape you possibly can. Those feelings and relationships will be strong "voices" inside you even long after your mom or dad may be gone.

Family One—Family Two

Working on "home improvement" is also important because Family One, the one you grow up in, is the only practice you get for Family Two, the mate and children you will one day call "my family." And as my sons found out in football and my daughter found out in band, if you don't get it right in practice, you will probably blow it in the Big One. We tend to replay what we did with Family One when we get to Family Two. Maybe that's one reason the Bible talks about "the sin of the fathers" being passed on to "the third and fourth generation" (Exodus 20:5). So, what kind of person do you want to be with your husband or wife, with your son or daughter someday? You need to start being that person right now with your mom and dad, with your brother and sister!

Ultimately, the reason for you playing your position well at home is the orders we have from God. He says, "Children, obey your parents in the Lord, for this is right. 'Honor your father and mother'—which is the first commandment with a promise—'that it may go well with you and that you may enjoy long life on the earth'" (Ephesians 6:1–3).

To put it simply, treat Mom and Dad right, and God will treat you right. He doesn't say, "Honor them if . . ." Your assignment is to honor them whether they are honorable or not. You do it "for this is right." Just as a private is ultimately obeying the general when he obeys his sergeant, so you are obeying God when you obey and honor your parents.

Jesus summed it all up in His command to "Do to others as you would have them do to you" (Luke 6:31). Notice—not as they do to you, that's *thermometer* living. It says, "as you would have them do to you." That's *thermostat* living! No longer will you say, "If you'll do what's right, I will." This is stepping up to say, "I'll do what's right—no matter what you do."

Five Power Sentences That Can Build Your Family

The following five sentences are a script for "home improvement." They are feelings that need to be expressed often from you to your mom, dad, and siblings.

Maybe these are words they have spoken a lot to you. Or they may be words that are seldom, if ever, said where you live. The less these feelings are expressed in your family, the more you need to express them!

When I was in elementary school, we used to show off by saying the longest word in the English language—"antidisestablishmentarianism." Of course, after you said it, your tongue had to take a couple days off. It was hard to say.

The good news is that these five power sentences all contain one-syllable words—they should be easy to say. But maybe they're not. For some reason, a lot of young people find it harder to say these simple, encouraging words than "antidisestablishmentarianism." But even if you are the only one saying these things—especially if you're the only one—they are the foundation on which healthy relationships are built. They're worth saying over and over again, even if they seem hard to say.

Power Sentence #1: "I Love You."

How often do the members of your family get an "I love you" from you, either in words or in actions? I can tell you how often they need to get it—every day! We human-types are funny that way. We don't experience life as years or months or even weeks—life is days to us. And each new day, there is a little voice inside each member of your family whispering, "Where do I stand today? Does she (or he) love me today?" It may be hard to imagine that your mother or father actually need your love—you may just be aware that you need theirs. But number of birthdays does not change a person's most basic emotional need—knowing they are loved by the people who are important to them. A parent who isn't sure of their son or daughter's love feels insecure, scared, inadequate—and often shows it in ways that make a teenager's life more difficult.

In spite of whatever frustrations and differences you may have, you probably do love your family—a lot. But the important question is, "Do they feel loved by you?" Go around the family circle and ask that about each one in it. If you are loved but don't feel loved, it feels the same as not being loved. Your parents, for example, will be deeply wounded people if they can't feel your love for them.

Communicating love is based on a fundamental realization. Imagine that you are sitting in the school library studying (I know, this requires a lot of imagination). Suddenly a frantic man runs into the library, screaming at the top of his lungs—in Russian. He is waving his arms wildly, and obviously he is trying to communicate important information. What he's trying to tell everyone is: "The school is on fire!" Now, the message is important, and the messenger is sincere. There's just one minor problem—he is not communicating in the language of the people who need to know!

Maybe that is why your family isn't totally getting the message that you love them—you're not loving them in their language. Every member of your family has their own language of love. Your mission is to make them feel loved by doing and saying the things that are their language of love.

So, what makes a parent feel loved? Here's a starter list.

Pitching In

Your mom and dad have to put a lot of time, effort, and sometimes money into keeping your home running—from garbage to cooking to housecleaning to yard work. The list is almost endless. When you offer to help with some of the chores, you say "I love you" in a very "feel-able" way.

Staying Home

When you always have someone else to be with and somewhere else to be, it's pretty tough for your mom or dad to feel loved by you. It means more to a parent than you will ever know for you to actually choose to spend time with them—and not just at official "family times."

Telling Them

You may not be the "I love you" type. Your family members may not seem like they are the "I love you" type. But each one of them needs to hear the words consistently! You can't just assume they know. If you don't tell them, they don't know. You can't just treat parents and siblings on the basis that "I love you 'til further notice. If I ever stop, you'll be the first to know." Silent love feels the same as missing love.

Touching Them

Hugs rule. Even if they aren't the type who show you affection in physical ways, they need that kind of love from you. After all, you're trying to change the climate, not just leave it where it's been, right?

Treating Them Well in Public

How do you treat your parents, brother, or sister in front of other people? If you treat them as if they are nonexistent or an embarrassment or a nuisance, you are wounding them badly. Love builds the other person up and never tears them down.

Doing the Little Thoughtful Things

Unscheduled, unrequested, unexpected little expressions that you care—a note, a call, a gift without an occasion, a chore without being asked. When you start looking for ways to love people in their language, you see lots of little kindnesses you can do to send the message.

Love that can be felt is almost never easy love. But then, a fast-food, Burger Barn Zippy Meal is easy, but it just isn't nearly as satisfying as the less-zippy, home-cooked dinner. A real meal takes time and work and someone going beyond what's "easy." So does real love. Your parents may be walking around with a hungry, empty spot in their heart because they are starved for some love from their son or daughter. And if you just try to communicate "I love you" in the ways that are easy for you, their heart-hunger probably will not be satisfied. Loving your family in their language almost always means going beyond what is "easy" to what is sacrifice.

Power Sentence #2: "Thank You."

Have you ever been kissed by a dolphin? "Not on porpoise," you say? Well, if you ever want to be kissed by a dolphin (now that's desperate!), just go to the dolphin show at Sea World and volunteer. You walk out onto a platform high above the pool and pucker up. Dolly Dolphin will start at the other end of the pool, jet-propel herself to the end where you are, do a flying, splashing leap into the air—and plant one on you!

Now as "yuk" as Dolly's kiss might sound to you, you have to be amazed that a dolphin can learn to do that! (After all, you may not exactly be Dolly's idea of a hot date either!) Actually, those Sea World dolphins do lots of amazing things such as throwing and catching a ball, dancing on their tails, and pole vaulting. The secret? The fish.

Every time Dolly does something good, she swims right back to the trainer in the corner. The trainer reaches into her bag and pulls out a reward—a delicious fish. And as long as Dolly keeps getting those rewards, she will keep doing the things that please her trainer.

Actually, "loving" parents is a lot like that. You can encourage them to do a lot of good things if you reward them when they do. But not with fish. With the power sentence "Thank you."

Appreciation may not be a very common experience in your home, but you can help change that. As a thermostat, you can make the cold a little warmer by making "thank you" a sentence you say every day. Becoming an appreciator can begin with some blank pieces of paper, one for each member of your family. First, put a family member's name at the top of each piece; then, you put these words in bold print at the top of each one's paper.

Things _____ (name) does because he/she loves me.

Try to make each person's list as long as you possibly can. Include the little things they do, not just the big ones. Think of things you may even take for granted. Then, your "make a difference" assignment is to begin regularly thanking them for those gifts and looking for others that come up each day.

If I asked you to make a list of the frustrating things each person did, you would probably request extra paper! But that's because we record the "wrongs" and forget the "rights."

When it comes to what you see in your family, you can focus on the ugly factors in them—or you can decide to focus on what's beautiful in them, even when you have to really look for it. A "thank you" life is one that chooses to focus on what's right with people, not what's wrong with them.

You can be a builder in your family if you look for the positive and say thanks for what you find. Your parents need praise. They need someone who will see the good in them and tell them. In many ways, your mom and dad are probably as unsure of themselves as you are. They are just better at covering it up. You can literally help them fill some of the gaps in their heart with statements such as these:

- "Thank you for being so generous."
- "Your sense of humor really cheers me up."
- "I really appreciate the little extras you do to make our house look nicer."
- "When you do that, it makes me feel special. Thanks."
- "I appreciate the sacrifices you make to be sure I have what I need."
- "It means a lot when you take time for me like this."
- "Thank you for pushing me to be the best I can be."

Those are just examples. The point is that you consciously look for traits or actions you can compliment and affirm—even if you only see an occasional glimmer of them. That is where the dolphin syndrome kicks in. If you like something in your parents, reward them with the "fish" of appreciation, and don't be surprised if they swim around the pool and do it again!

And don't wait for the funeral. Some day you will stand where I stood some years ago—beside your parent's casket. It was too late for me to say thanks to my dad anymore—and I had a lot to thank him for. I just hope you won't make the mistake of waiting for the funeral to start thinking and saying what you appreciate about your mom, dad, sister, or brother. They need to hear it now!

Power Sentence #3: "How Do You Feel?"

You're speed-talking to a friend and suddenly you lose your train of thought in the middle of a sentence. You ask your friend for a little help—"Uh, what was I saying?" Watch their face. The mouth drops open, the eyes widen and start darting back and forth, looking for an escape, and then the answer you have heard 99 out of 100 times—"I have no idea."

Nobody listens. At least, that's the way it feels most of the time. And it sure feels that way in the average home! You may look around your family and say, "Nobody listens to anybody here." Why don't you decide to change it? "Nobody *understands* around here." Then, change it!

Our natural tendency is to want everyone else to understand how we feel. But a family "make a difference" person decides to reverse that by always pursuing this question—"How do you feel?" If you want to improve things at home, make up your mind to become the Chief Listener there and the Chief Understander (we don't understand a person because we don't listen to them). And decide to look for the needs that are underneath a person's deeds.

It all begins with listening. God's simple, powerful blueprint for healthy relationships is that "everyone should be quick to listen, slow to speak and slow to become angry" (James 1:19). The question is—do those words describe your communication with your family? Are you quick to listen—or quick to speak? Are you slow to speak—or slow to listen? And if you talk first and listen later, you are probably quick, not slow, to become angry. An unlistening, unsympathizing person helps turn a home into a battlefield. A listening, caring person helps turn a home into a harbor.

You can make a difference if you stop to find out "how do you feel?" before you do much talking. This caring, understanding lifestyle includes at least three positive action steps.

1. Try to walk in their shoes.

You may look at your father's wing tips and say, "No way I'm wearing those things!" Understood. But it's a walk in their emotional shoes that matters. What is it Dad's feeling because of what's going on at work? What does he do there anyway? What pressures are squeezing Mom in her responsibilities right now? What went on in their growing-up years that might be making them act or feel this way? What does it feel like to be at this stage of their life right now? When they nag me like this, what's really going on inside them? What are they really trying to say? How does it make them feel when I'm like this?

2. Include them.

Parents nag when they feel excluded from a life they gave birth to. Parents trust when they feel included by their son or daughter. You can win their trust by volunteering to tell them where you're going, what your plans are, what happened at school today, what your friends are like, what you're going through—even bad news that could get you in.trouble. They will respect you for telling them; they will distrust you if they find it out another way. When you let your parents into your life, they don't have to keep banging on the door to get in, and you are understanding one of their greatest needs—the need to be included in your life. Talking builds trust. Silence breeds suspicion.

3. Ask their opinion.

It's smart to get your parents' viewpoint on what is going on in your life. First, because you're going to get their opinion anyway! You might as well build some bridges by asking for it rather than waiting for them to volunteer it. Second, it's smart to ask their opinion for the same reason I might seek advice about a trip to China from someone who's been there—they have seen and experienced what I'm about to see and experience. And the third reason for seeking your parents' ideas is the most important—because God says to do it! "Listen ... to your father's instruction and do not forsake your mother's teaching.... Pay attention and gain understanding" (Proverbs 1:8; 4:1).

It is important for you to try to find out what's going on in your mom or dad's heart before you respond. Listening to their words alone may not give you the whole picture—you need to listen for their heart. When you become the "how do you feel?" person in your family, you become a heart specialist. And you can bring a lot of hope and a lot of healing.

Power Sentence #4: "I Was Wrong."

Fonzie used to try to say this sentence on *Happy Days*. He knew he had blown it—so he agonizingly started into those words, "I was—wrooooo—I was wro-wro-wro—." Then, in one last painful rush—"I was wr-wr-WRONG!"

Fonzie's not the only one who has a hard time getting those words out. Almost everyone does—especially at home! Nobody wants to admit they were wrong. No one wants to feel like they lost ... that he or she is the weak one. But the ironic truth is this—it is the strong person who can admit they were wrong.

There may well be a voice inside you objecting, "I'm not about to apologize—nobody is ever wrong at our house!" Thermometer. That kind of "I'll just reflect the temperature everyone else sets" approach just makes the family a harder, more polarized place to live. But when a young person decides to be a thermostat—to "do to others as you would have them do to you"—some healing can finally begin to replace the hurting. Peace talks can be scheduled where there were only battles before. God gives us an important key to relationships that work when He tells us, "Confess your sins to each other and pray for each other so that you may be healed" (James 5:16).

"I was wrong" are three of the most healing words in the English language. How many walls could come down—or be avoided—if you would step up to be the apologizer, the forgiver, the wrong-righter of your family?

If your mom or dad frustrates you with their need to always be right, you can almost be sure they grew up around that kind of pride and rigidity. Their mother or father was like that—and your mom or dad picked it up like a thermometer instead of seeing how frustrating it was and changing it. You may be at the same crossroads right now. Twenty years from now, will your son or daughter be going crazy because you can never be wrong? You know how a "never wrong" person makes a child feel. Now is your opportunity to decide to be different. If you don't, you will reproduce the very rigidity you hate.

Ultimately, the person who can say "I was wrong" in a family is the emotionally healthiest person there—because a healthy person does not care who is right. He or she only cares about what is right—no matter whether that makes them the "winner" or the "loser."

When you live like that in "practice," you are laying a foundation for great respect when you have a family of your own.

Power Sentence #5: "I Need Help."

It's hard to believe there was a time when you couldn't burp by yourself. When you think about how well you do it now, it seems strange that you ever needed a parent thumping your back to get a burp out. They were pleased when you burped then. They are not pleased when you burp now. Funny creatures, these parent people.

Of course, there was a time you couldn't feed yourself, too—and that's really hard to imagine when you consider how very well you're doing with that now. You couldn't walk without help, turn over without help, even get out of the mess you made after you ate! Basically, we were all cute little losers there for the first few months. We couldn't do what we needed to do without some help.

That's still true whenever a young person decides to change the kind of son or daughter they are. Any time you decide to make a difference, the difference always has to start with you. You ask yourself, "What things do I need to work on in me to help change the climate in this family?"

It may be a negative attitude, a sarcastic mouth, an unappreciative spirit, a selfish outlook—but whatever it is, a young person needs help and support in order to grow. Compared to changing destructive habits and attitudes, those burping and feeding challenges were easy!

So the five powerful sentences that can build your family culminate with three last words that can open your parents' hearts to a new beginning—"I need help." Actually, the heart-opening begins when you risk that other healing sentence, "I was wrong." Having admitted that you have made some mistakes, you now reach out to your family, asking them to help you and support you as you try to be a better son or daughter, a better brother or sister. It may sound something like this:

I really want the rest of our days together to be the best of our days. And in order for that to happen, I know there are some things I need to work on. I've been too _____, I haven't been _____ enough. I've made things more tense here by _____. I think I may have hurt you sometimes by the way I _____.

I really want to work at making our family an even better place to be. But I can't do this alone. I need your help. Give me a chance to change and grow. Gently remind me when you see the old me showing up again. Forgive me when I mess up and pray for me.

Just put yourself in your mom or dad's spot for a minute, and imagine hearing words like these from your son or daughter. Imagine how it would make you feel toward your child about your relationship, maybe even about your own weaknesses and failings. There are no guaranteed reactions to any of these power sentences, but they have the potential to really open up new and better relationships.

In our house, the thermometer does not immediately jump up to seventy degrees as soon as I set the thermostat on that temperature—there's a time lag between the time a new temperature is set and the time the house heats up. It is the same way when a son or daughter decides to live like a thermostat in their family. You may be doing your "I love you" and your "thank you" and "I was wrong" and other sentences for quite a while before you see any change in the climate at home. But if you will be consistent and patient, the new temperature you are setting with your life is likely to begin spreading throughout the house.

One way to start a process of change in your family is for you to write a letter to your parents. The letter has four main subjects. I can give you the outline, but you have to make it yours. Your "Dear Mom and Dad" letter should include these ideas:

"I love you ..."

"Thank you for ..."

Here's where you express your appreciation for all the positive things they are and they do.

"I'm sorry for ..."

You can start a healing process by writing down any actions or attitudes that may have hurt them.

"I wish we could ..."

Tell Mom and Dad about how you would like your relationship to be for the rest of your days together.

Why a letter? Because you will probably say it better if you don't have the interruptions and sidetracks of a conversation. Also, they will probably receive it better if they don't have to respond to you as they would in a conversation. Besides, they will only hear what you say once; they may read what you write several times! At the end of your letter, you may want to tell your parents that you would like to talk about what you wrote if they would like to. That could set the stage for a powerful and important time together.

When You're Sick of Winter

The morning I woke up to three feet of snow, it looked as if we would have snow in our yard forever! And I'm not very tall—I almost disappear in three feet of snow! When a plow finally came to dig us out, he piled the snow in mountains that looked like wanna-be Alps. Then it snowed again! Would it always be winter? Of course not. I only had to think about one little word—spring—and I had hope. Hope is knowing that it won't always be like this—that something better is coming.

Hope is ultimately the word this chapter has been all about—hope that your family doesn't have to be what it has always been, that something better is possible. The thaw begins when you decide that with Jesus' help you can and you will be the "Make A Difference" person for your family. Making those five power sentences part of the life of your family, you have hope that things can be better. It doesn't have to stay winter. You can help introduce spring.

5 Running Without Baggage

TICKING TIME BOMB #5:

Letting the Pain of the Past Poison Your Future

My kids had no idea. We were just sitting around the living room talking about "stuff"—and I had a tape recorder running. You can get arrested for doing this on the telephone—but my family has decided not to press charges against me.

That doesn't mean they are excited about the tapes. After all, Lisa was only about five at the time, Doug about three, and Brad a babbling one-year-old. Lisa is talking a lot on the tape, Doug is praying that Jesus will "bless Mommy, truck, Barbie," and Brad is speaking some language as yet unknown to man. We have a lot of laughs when we play back that tape.

Then there is the tape of our wedding those lonnnnggg years ago. Karen was young and beautiful. I was young and dorky—but we were—and still are—two people very much in love. You can tell by listening to the tape. Sometimes on our anniversary we pull out that tape and listen to what we promised each other on the day our marriage began. It's Kleenex time.

Some great memories are recorded on those tapes. But not all tapes are like that. Richard Nixon found that out. While he was president of the United States, he had a recorder secretly installed to tape every conversation in the Oval Office. Nobody knew about those tapes until a scandal broke over a politically motivated break-in at the Watergate Hotel in Washington, D.C. Suddenly those tapes became evidence of conspiracies and illegal actions that were going on at the White House—and of an unflattering side of the president that most people had never heard. Eventually, Richard Nixon had to resign from the presidency. If he were still alive today, he would probably tell you that not all tapes are good tapes.

Memories of kids growing up and the wedding promises of a young couple in love—good tapes. Men belittling other people, planning illegal activities, spitting out angry profanities—ugly tapes. Whether the recollections are good or ugly, tapes keep bringing them back for an encore.

The recorder we have in our brain must run on Energizer Bunny batteries—it just keeps going and going and going. So we keep replaying the experiences of our lives, both the good and the ugly. From the time there was a you, your personal "recorder" has been storing the feelings, words, and experiences of your life—including your painful times. It may have been the angry words of your parents' arguments or the sounds of their marriage coming apart—or the hard times their divorce caused you. The recorder may have picked up the unspeakable trauma of physical or sexual abuse against you, or of the tragic loss of someone you loved, or the hurt of losing a relationship that was important to you. The tapes may carry the pain that a tragedy, illness, or injury caused you.

Or even some things that you did that you are not very proud of.

Whatever the hurt, it just seems to keep on replaying without you ever hitting a "play" button. And each day, the tape keeps running, recording whatever new hurts are piling on the old ones.

Because of the collapse of so many families and because people seem to be wounding each other more and more, the P.Q. (Pain Quotient) of the young generation seems to be higher than it has ever been. A lot of kids are carrying a lot of hurt—you may be one of them.

Much of who you are and what you do may be a result of how you have been hurt. When I am having one of my "bad back" days, everyone can tell. Even though only one part of my body is hurting, the rest of my body is bent all out of shape. Emotional pain in one part of your life can have a similar effect on your personality, your emotions, your attitude—it can bend the rest of your life out of shape.

It would be difficult to put yourself on a couch and psychoanalyze yourself, pen and notepad in hand—"So what do you think makes you be that way? What do you think makes you feel that way?" But you can be sure that the experiences that hurt you in the past—the ones that insist on replaying—can really shape who you are.

The hard truth is you probably had no choice about the pain that has come into your life—you may very well have been the victim of someone else's sins and problems. But the hard truth also is that you do have a choice about how you handle that hurt. And that choice will shape your future much more than the person or experience that hurt you.

Unless you deal with the pain, it will begin to morph into anger and bitterness, self-pity and self-centeredness, negativism and depression. And in the center of your soul this ugly hard spot will start to grow—a hostile emotional desert inside you. The ugly tapes will grow loudspeakers that will blare all over the people around you. Without realizing it, the hurtee—that's you—will start to become the hurter.

But if you deal with the pain constructively, you can defuse the emotional time bomb that has leveled so many young people—letting the pain of your past ruin your future.

You can't do anything about the past—it cannot be rewritten. It happened, and it hurt. But your future is yet to be written. And it really is up to you if the pain has a future or not. The question is—will you do what it takes to bury those ugly tapes and begin to make some new tapes to build the future on? The old tapes have been played enough. The pain has done enough damage. It's time to move on.

No Fun to Run with Bertha

"Bertha needs to go to Jenny Craig." That is what I often tell the agent at the airport when Bertha and I are checking in for our flight. No, Bertha does not let me have it. Bertha is not a relative or friend or coworker—she is my often overstuffed garment bag/suitcase. We spend so much time together traveling that I decided to give her a name. Which sometimes causes the agent to excuse herself for a moment and call for backup help.

Sometimes, because I am basically carrying my office with me and even supplies for the events I am headed for, Bertha is really jammed, and she has two or three other suitcases for company. Obviously, I want to check them so the baggage handlers get to carry them instead of me. But every once in a while, the baggage handlers get a break—and I get a hernia. There have been those times when I was running late. And there was no time to check Bertha and the Baggage Company. You would enjoy a video of me galumphing through the airport with suitcases hanging all over my body. Don't get excited—no such video exists. If it did, it would self-destruct in ten seconds, "Mission Impossible" style. Believe me, it is like Mission Impossible trying to run full speed when you are carrying a lot of baggage!

Maybe that's what is slowing you down—you are trying to run full speed emotionally, but all that baggage from the past is really slowing you down. The pain, the memories, the weight of all that has happened can make life feel a lot heavier. That is why it is so important that you learn how you can unload the baggage of the past, how you can let go of the pain.

When you hang onto the pain of your past—when you try to run with all that baggage, it has several consequences that make the load even heavier.

You Sink into the Swamp of Self

When you feel like a victim in life, it is easy to become a self-focused, self-centered person, always thinking about yourself. If you focus on how you have been hurt, your life-script tends to have a lot of complaining, "poor me" talk in it. And the attendance at pity parties is usually pretty low—like one person. A self-focused person tends to drive other people away—and then complain about how people treat them. But thinking and talking about yourself most of the time is like emotional bad breath—nobody wants to get close to it. Which compounds the hurt of the past with isolation in the present.

"But I really am hurting ... do I just stuff it inside?" No! There is Someone who will never tire of hearing your hurts. Here is God's better idea—"I cry aloud to the Lord; I lift up my voice to the Lord for mercy. I pour out my complaint before him; before him I tell my trouble" (Psalm 142:1–2).

There is a place to cry, to pour out your complaints, to tell your trouble—in the loving presence of the Lord. He welcomes our deepest heart-cries. He will understand because He has been there, and He will bring a sense of peace and well-being if you leave it with Him. What good does it do to dump your complaints and your pain on all those other people? It just makes them back off when you need them to be close. Why not leave your troubles in Hands that can do something about them!

Someone might say, "Well, I pray about what's hurting me, but it doesn't help." Well, praying about what is hurting doesn't help if all you do is tell God about it. You have to *leave* it with Him! When you leave your baggage with God, you do not have to ask everyone else around you to carry it. In fact, maybe you can even help someone else carry theirs.

Escape on Runaway Road

In addition to sinking into the swamp of self, hanging onto your pain can also cause another damaging effect ...

you escape on Runaway Road. When you have given up on a cure for your pain, you are tempted to settle for a little pain relief, to run away from it with a party, a bottle, a drug, a sexual relationship—even with suicide, the most expensive escape of all. Tragically, the results of the pain reliever often just create more pain than you had before.

When you try to drown your sorrows, you often end up drowning *you*. The problem with Runaway Road is that it is a circle—you keep running into what you are running from. Only it keeps getting bigger the longer you wait to deal with it. Denial ultimately increases the very pain you are trying to escape.

Untying Your Leg

When I was a kid, our church had a picnic every year. I ate enough fried chicken to start cackling when I laughed. I also loved the games that involved everybody from the pastor to the grandmas to the parents to the brats like me. I remember one event that was always good for laughs—the three-legged race. You and your partner had to run this course with your right leg and his left leg tied together. I don't exactly run like an Olympic medalist when I use both my legs—but this stumble/bumble three-legged stuff made me a finalist for "Klutz of the Year." It is hard to run when you are tied to someone else who is slowing you down!

And that is the problem when the pain of the past leads to another hurtful consequence . . . you activate the bitter bomb. In other words, you let anger and resentment and bitterness fester in your heart toward the people who hurt you—the ones who abandoned you, betrayed you, abused you, belittled you, neglected you. But when that happens, you actually end up tied to the very person you want to be away from—your grudge makes you think about them a lot. And it is hard to run when you are tied to someone who is slowing you down. Unfortunately, when you harbor bitterness toward someone, you cannot get away from that person emotionally!

God warns us of the greater pain that results from allowing our hurt to become bitterness. "See to it that no one misses the grace of God and that no bitter root grows up to cause trouble and defile many" (Hebrews 12:15).

One resource you cannot afford to be without if your pain is ever going to heal is the grace of God. But the Bible says that grace cannot go where bitterness lives. You forfeit so much of the help God wants to give you when you force out His grace with your bitterness. Your hard feelings probably are not bothering your hurter much at all … but they are eating you up inside!

And if you do not deal with that resentment, that bitterness, maybe even that hate, it will be like a time bomb inside you. Those feelings will explode onto other people who haven't hurt you, probably people you love. Unresolved bitterness really does "cause trouble and defile many." But the "trouble" is usually trouble for you and the "many" are usually people you care about, not the people who hurt you.

Why, God?

One of the most devastating mistakes hurting people make is to avoid God, forget God, or even turn their back on God. Somehow, they direct their anger and resentment at their Creator and forfeit His help at the very time they need it most.

One question that seems to arise when we are hit with tragedy or loss is, "Why, God?" And that is understandable. In our pain, we want to make some sense out of this senseless occurrence, get some answers from the only One who knows "why." But because we are seventy-year wonders trying to figure out a plan that stretches across eternity, we seldom get satisfying answers to the "why" question.

My friend Joe works with teenagers in Beirut, Lebanon, a city that has had terrible civil war and bloodshed. He told me how his church was emotionally devastated when one of their gifted young leaders was killed by a stray shell while walking near his house. And in their grief and confusion, everyone wanted that same answer we want in hurting times. But at the funeral, the pastor of that church said something very profound as he poured out his heart. He said, "We are all asking, 'Why, God?'— and I would like an answer to that myself. But we probably won't know why until we are in heaven and can see the whole plan. But perhaps there is a better question for us to be asking right now—'How can God use this?'"

That really is a better question—because that has answers that we can understand, that we can act on. God—and God alone—has the amazing ability to make something that is garbage into gold. The Bible simply promises that "in all things God works for the good of those who love him" (Romans 8:28).

The Bible did not say "all things are good." What happened to you was not good—in fact, it may have even been because of something that is sin in God's eyes. But no matter how terrible, how evil, how painful, how "senseless" it is, God can make good come from it. And that is how you will be able to make some sense out of the senseless, some peace out of the confusion.

Running from God because of your pain takes you away from the only hope of any healing, any help, any meaning. With all your anger, all your confusion, all your exploding feelings, run *to* God, not away from Him. He can handle your feelings ... but you can't—without Him.

The first step to putting the pain of the past behind you is to stop doing the things that will increase the pain. You cannot decide whether or not you have the hurt. But you can decide you will not sink in self-pity, run into denial, let bitterness take over, or avoid Jesus, the only One who can rebuild you.

Beautiful Garbage

Your mother went through a lot when you were being born into this world—a fact she may have mentioned to "motivate" you every once in a while. Women do endure a great deal to have a baby. The process is painful. But my wife, Karen, went back two more times after Lisa for an encore. And Doug and Brad are glad she did. Millions of women have chosen to repeat that painful process. Why? Because the result is beautiful (you may now go look in the mirror and admire yourself).

The way God works at the beginning of life is often the way He works throughout your life. He allows—and occasionally sends—painful events to come into your life. While you are going through it, there is nothing beautiful about it. Like labor pains, it just hurts. But the same

God who brings something beautiful, something so worth having out of that pain, can do the same with yours. No tragedy, no trauma, no crime, no injustice, no betrayal is so awful that the all-powerful God cannot give birth to new life from it.

No incident in the history of Planet Earth was more ugly, more wrong than the brutal torture and execution of God's sinless Son, Jesus. It was obscene. It was unspeakable evil. But out of the ugliest act ever committed by humankind, God brought the most beautiful miracle in the universe—He tore down the wall between us and Him and made heaven possible for everyone He created.

However devastating and painful your experience may have been, it cannot be as ugly as the one and only Son of God, murdered on a cross, carrying the hell of billions of people. If God can bring incredible good out of that, couldn't He bring something beautiful out of the things that have caused your pain?

He can—if you let Him. If you are willing to let go of the pain of your past so you do not have to carry it into your future. Then the only question is, "How do I let go of that pain? How can I unload this baggage from the past?" The answer begins with four steps to healing.

Four Steps to Healing

Healing Step #1: Face Your Pain with Some People Who Support You

Drowning people know what to do. They instinctively yell that simple little word that is their last, best hope—HEL-LLLPPPP! Their cry for help alerts people to their predicament and brings someone who can make a difference.

In a way, trying to survive the pain of your past is like drowning. You cannot get out of this alone. You do not have to rescue yourself, but you do have to yell "help." So many young people are suffering needlessly—going under emotionally—because they will not let anyone know about the predicament they are in. In fact, some of that suffering is because they will not even face the fact of their pain and what is causing it.

Sometimes the monster that caused the pain is so ugly that you just want to run from it. Many issues are like that, but none more than the monster of sexual abuse. Perhaps no sin is more twisted, more devastating to its victim than this one. And researchers estimate that as many as one out of three women has been sexually abused—and possibly as many men. So, many teenagers and adults are walking around with this awful scar, this ticking time bomb inside. When it goes off, it can express itself in the form of sexual promiscuity, homosexuality, suicidal tendencies, eating disorders, emotional hardness, depression—a lot of ugly aftermaths.

Often these behaviors or lifestyles develop because the abuse victim has been made to feel like trash—which you throw away, right? They don't realize that they are God's workmanship from birth—that no one on earth gave them their worth, and no one on earth can take it away—including an abuser. Ironically, the abuse victim often carries around this voice inside that says, "You're to blame" (which the abuser may have even told them) when, in fact, they are a victim, trapped and exploited by someone they trusted. And having been betrayed by someone they trusted, abuse victims are often afraid of close relationships—so they settle for the "safety" of relationships that are superficial.

God hates sexual abuse. He said in His law, "No one is to approach any close relative to have sexual relations" (Leviticus 18:6). Then He told the Israelites what should happen to people who did things like these—"Everyone who does any of these detestable things—such persons must be cut off from their people" (Leviticus 18:29).

Given the ugliness of sexual abuse, it is no wonder a victim would rather live in denial than face it. But given the damage sexual abuse does when it is not dealt with, it is simply too devastating not to face it. If you are a silent victim of sexual abuse, you need to yell "help" before it drowns you. There are counselors at church, at school, in clinics who have faced this monster with many people like you. Your healing will begin the day you face it with someone who can support you.

Your wounds may come from a different source—trouble in your family, heartbreak in your relationships, grief over a terrible loss, depression from a major trauma or hurt. Whatever the cause of the pain baggage you are carrying, one principle stands at the entrance of the road to healing ... you have to face your pain to fix your pain. Ignoring it does not make it go away—it just makes it go deeper. So whatever the risks of facing this monster, the risks of not facing it are much greater.

Why try to carry that baggage alone when "two are better than one.... If one falls down, his friend can help him up.... Though one may be overpowered, two can defend themselves" (Ecclesiastes 4:9–10, 12). Sometimes when I am running through an airport, decorated with heavy baggage all over my body, I have a friend with me. He offers to help carry what is too heavy for me to run with. With someone else sharing my load, I can go a lot farther, a lot faster. So can you.

Facing your pain is the first step on the road to healing your pain. The next step is a challenging one—but one that has amazing power to set you free.

Healing Step #2: Forgive the People Who Hurt You

"I hate this book!" this girl says. "It scares me. It disgusts me. It makes me stressed."

The surprising thing is that she is now reading that book for the tenth time! The logical question seems to be, "If you hate it so much, why do you keep reading it over and over?" Isn't it about time she puts that book on the shelf once and for all and starts another book?

That is the kind of choice the Bible has in mind when it uses the healing word, *forgive*.

Forgiveness is not a feeling; it's a choice. You decide to quit reading again and again the volume of your life called "The Hurting Times" and begin a new volume based on the future, not the past. Of course, Volume 1 has a villain or two in it—the people who caused your pain. In order to start a new volume, you will have to deal with your feelings toward your hurters—or you will poison Volume 2 with them.

"It's impossible." That is the way many people feel about forgiving someone who wronged them. And it is impossible—without the help of the Great Forgiver. He is the One who said of the people who had just nailed Him to a cross, "Father, forgive them." He did not give them what they deserved. He asked for what they did not deserve—forgiveness. This same Jesus can give His for-give-ability to anyone who sincerely comes to Him for it.

"It's not right to just let them off the hook—not after what they did to me." That feeling is very understandable, even logical. But judging and punishing is God's job, not ours. He says, "It is mine to avenge; I will repay" (Romans 12:19).

Letting the people who hurt you off the hook—or not letting them off the hook—is up to God, and He will do a much better job of enforcing justice than you ever could. Forgiving someone is not denying the wrong they did or pretending that it was okay. It is releasing what they did to God and deciding not to make the way they treated you the basis for the way you treat them.

The reality is that you are tied to that hurter until you forgive him or her. When you let the offender go, you are letting yourself go! You forgive those who caused you pain, not because they deserve it, but because you need to release them and open yourself up for the healing Jesus can do only in a forgiver's heart. The healing can continue when you break the chain of bitterness and resentment and anger that has bound you to someone who wounded you.

Forgiveness is radical—and God tells us how we can pull off this liberating step—"Forgive whatever griev-ances you may have against one another. Forgive as the Lord forgave you" (Colossians 3:13). Forgiving is a deci-sion to treat your hurter, not as they treated you, but as Jesus treated you. And we certainly did not deserve His forgiveness. It was our sinning that made Him go to that cross. When you decide to begin treating those who have caused your pain as Jesus has treated you—who caused His pain—you are ready for your new beginning. You have just put that repulsive old volume on the shelf forever and started page one of a brand-new volume.

The next step on the road to healing actually moves you from being the victim to being a healer yourself.

Healing Step #3: Find Some People Who Need You

One of the best ways to move beyond your pain is to help others move beyond theirs. And because of what you have been through, you have something to give other wounded people.

Like Tom, for example. He was listening to my radio program, "Alive! with Ron Hutchcraft," one night in his room in Kansas. The subject was loneliness that night—a subject Tom knew a lot about. In fact, he had experienced so much rejection and loneliness that he was considering suicide that night. In a wonderful way, Jesus came into Tom's room—and into his heart—through his radio that night and changed his life. I did not know about that miracle until a couple of years later when I met Tom. He was a student at a Bible school and a counselor at the youth outreach I was speaking for. Tom told me about how Jesus had touched him that night ... and about what he was living for now. "I know what loneliness feels like," he explained, "and I decided to spend the rest of my life reaching out to other lonely people." Tom had taken a major step toward healing—turning the pain of his life into caring for others in pain.

That is the lifestyle Jesus had in mind when He said, "Whoever wants to save his life will lose it, but whoever loses his life for me will save it" (Luke 9:24). Unloading the baggage of your pain means leaving the "swamp of self" where a lot of hurting people live and becoming an "others" person instead. And like Tom, it is the garbage of your life that will qualify you to be a "Make A Difference" person. If you let Jesus do His garbage miracle.

With a process called recycling, human engineers have figured out ways to take garbage and turn it into something useful. That is why on two Tuesday nights a month, I get to haul all our newspapers, empty bottles, and jars out to the street. The Recycling Fairy comes and our trash disappears—to be made into some more useful stuff.

Now it was not some human engineer who invented recycling. God has been in the recycling process since the beginning of time—taking the trash of people's lives and remaking it into something useful, something beautiful. That is what He did with Tom's years of rejection and loneliness when Tom let God recycle it into compassion for other lonely people.

God's "compassion chain" works like this—"The Father of compassion and the God of all comfort ... comforts us in all our troubles, so that we can comfort those in any trouble with the comfort we ourselves have received from God" (2 Corinthians 1:3–4).

It is so exciting to think that all the ugly things that have happened to you are not for nothing—God can recycle them into sensitivity, compassion, and maturity in you if you let go of your hurt and give it to "the Father of compassion ... the God of all comfort."

That is how it worked for Julie. She had been repeatedly abused sexually by two male family members. In
one instance, they had even used her to demonstrate the
facts of life to her cousin—who is a homosexual today.
But one day, in her early twenties, Julie faced the pain she
had been denying. Then, with supernatural help from
Jesus Christ, she was able to forgive the men who had so
wounded her. And today, Julie is a youth pastor's wife
with an incredible ministry to young women who—you
can probably guess—are sexual abuse victims. They listen to her because she has been there. And she understands their pain because she has been there. She can
help lead them out of their pain because she has been
there—and been healed! And some of her healing has
come from finding some people who she could help heal.

It will work the same way for you. The people who
need you may or may not have been through exactly what
you have been through. They may be homeless people,
sick people, rejected people, excluded people, street
people, handicapped people—but you will know what
hurt is, and you will have a great gift of love to give them.

Healing Step #4: Focus on the Person Who Can Fix You

He is a carpenter by trade. As a boy, He probably
started in His father's carpenter shop in Nazareth, learn-
ing to build and rebuild furniture. Today, He is Jesus the
Savior—and He rebuilds broken people. It is Jesus alone
who can touch the bleeding memories of your past and
begin to heal them.

For you to experience His power in your pain, you
have to focus on Him instead of your problem. If you do,

His promise to you is "You [God] will keep in perfect peace him whose mind is steadfast, because he trusts in you" (Isaiah 26:3).

There is something about suffering that can bring you deeper into Jesus than you have ever been before. Those who know the most about Jesus and His power are usually those who have hurt the most—because pain makes you desperate for Him. And desperate people open themselves up to the Lord in ways that people without pain may never know. When you totally open yourself up to Him, His love and His power come rushing into your life in ways only the wounded have tasted.

It actually can be worth all the hurt if it takes you into the central love and power of God Himself. The pain will last a little while. The relationship with God will last forever.

You can anchor yourself to that relationship by beginning each new day with Jesus. You can meet Him in the love letter He wrote to you—it's called the Bible. In that book are hundreds of promises of how God will love and protect you. If you memorize some of those words from God, you can have them in your heart for the hurting times. Spending time with Him each day and hanging onto His promises are keys to keeping your eyes on the Problem-Solver instead of on the problems. And focusing on this Caring Carpenter is where the rebuilding of a wounded you really begins.

6 Volcano Land

TICKING TIME BOMB #6:
Letting Your Anger Control You Instead of You
Controlling Your Anger

Flat.

That's what the scenery looked like where I grew up in Illinois. I thought a mountain was somebody's sloping driveway.

So I was blown away the first time I saw the Rocky Mountains. The view from 14,000 feet was awesome! Of course, I sounded like I was hyperventilating—not from excitement over the mountains, but because someone must have sucked up all the oxygen at that altitude!

Having seen the majesty of the Rockies, I thought I had seen mountains at their most mountainous. Wrong. I took a trip to Ecuador a few years ago and stayed with some friends whose house is surrounded by an incredible view of the mountains—including one called Mt. Antisana ... 19,000 feet high! This was the first time I had seen a mountain that could call one of those Rockies "junior."

I was even more amazed when my friend told me that scientists believe that peak used to be 10,000 feet higher! My reaction—"Used to be? What happened?"

Simple answer—"Antisana blew its top." Like many of the mountains in Ecuador, Antisana was a volcano. And they believe it had a massive explosion at one time—and literally blew its top. The explosion probably did not last very long, and it was a long time ago—but the damage the explosion left is there for good.

Actually, the same thing happens when you blow your top. There's the explosion, then the damage it leaves, then the scars on you and other people that may be there for years to come. And when we explode, it is usually the people we love the most who we hurt the most.

Two-legged volcanoes—that is what we are a lot of times. You can feel the emotional lava building inside you until—sooner or later—it really goes off. More and more young people seem to be carrying a growing anger inside them. That may be one reason many teenagers are attracted to music that is angry and defiant—an angry song shouts the dark feelings inside a lot of people.

And the young world can often be volcano country, where people are touchy and ready to "blow" over seemingly small frustrations. I recently asked a veteran high school teacher how kids have changed over the last twenty years. He quickly said, "The anger—I've never seen so many students carrying so much anger. And now kids get really upset over even small things. And they get real angry real fast ... they'll even start hitting ... even guys hitting girls."

One teenager told me, "There's a darkness inside me that scares me." Maybe you know that feeling—the ticking time bomb of anger inside you. How can you defuse its explosive power before it does any more damage?

First, you have to want to tame it. And you probably will not decide to fight the anger monster until you realize the damage your temper is causing—damage that can last long after the explosion and the reason for it is over.

The Bill for Blowing Your Top

We will never try to control our anger until we realize the damage it is doing to other people—often the people we love the most. Your anger puts scars on people, often lasting scars. We all carry tapes in our heart that have recorded things that have been said to us and about us over the years. You probably have some of the angry words of others on your tapes—and those words keep playing back, wounding you again with their slicing edge. As the Bible says, "Reckless words pierce like a sword" (Proverbs 12:18).

In spite of how the anger of others has "pierced" us, we continue to attack other people with our angry words. How many people close to you are carrying your wounding words on the tapes in their hearts? And how many more times will you scar them with your out-of-control temper?

The wounder may not even remember saying those hurting words—but the woundee may never forget them. You won't try to tame your personal volcano until you face the damage it is doing to people you care about.

You also begin to fight the battle against your anger when you realize how much blowing your top diminishes you. If the scientists are right, Mt. Antisana lost about 10,000 feet of itself when it blew. When you "lose it" emotionally, you really do lose—people's respect, people's trust—you may even lose the relationship itself. When you cannot control your temper, people think less of you, and, like that Ecuadorian volcano, you just do not stand as tall as you did before the eruptions.

So, those out-of-control blowups hurt people you care about, and they hurt you. There is someone else who gets wounded, too—someone you might not even think about. Your anger can actually make God cry. Speaking of God's sorrow, the Bible tells us—"Do not grieve the Holy Spirit of God" (Ephesians 4:30).

When people grieve, it often means tears. And apparently, something we can do so breaks God's heart that He actually grieves—cries—over it. To figure out what that is, you have to read what God says right before and right after this statement about His grief. The verse before says, "Do not let any unwholesome talk come out of your mouths, but only what is helpful for building others up.... Do not grieve the Holy Spirit" (Ephesians 4:29–30).

So whatever makes God cry has something to do with "unwholesome talk" coming out of our mouths. If the opposite is "what is helpful for building others up," then unwholesome talk must be talk that tears people down. The verse after the "grieving the Holy Spirit" statement defines trash talk—talk that trashes the other person—"Get rid of all bitterness, rage and anger, brawling and slander, along with every form of malice" (Ephesians 4:31).

Angry words. Cutting words. Bitter words. Those are the kinds of outbursts that make God cry.

Why do our "volcanic eruptions" hurt God? Because we are tearing down someone He is trying to build—and it makes God cry. In a sense, God has to repair the person we hurt before He can continue building them into the person He wants them to be.

So, just like an erupting volcano or a ticking time bomb, our temper can do serious damage—to people we love, to our self-respect and reputation, and even to God's heart. The explosions cost too much. We have to find a way to defuse this dark side of us. One of life's most expensive mistakes is letting your temper control you instead of you controlling your temper.

Emptying out your anger on people is a short-term emotional release that feels good for a little while. But the long-range effects of an out-of-control temper can take you farther from the people you care about and the person you want to be than you could ever imagine. And the longer you wait to get your temper under control, the more of a slave you become to your anger.

So, the time is now to face the fire inside you and bring it under control. An active volcano can eventually become a dormant volcano. A temper can be tamed.

Temper Taming

He must have been scary— the kind of man you don't want to meet on a dark street some night. He was literally a wild man.

We do not know his name, but the Bible lets us know how dangerous and uncontrollable he was. "A man with an evil spirit came from the tombs to meet him [Jesus]. This man lived in the tombs, and no one could bind him any more, not even with a chain. For he had often been chained hand and foot, but he tore the chains apart and broke the irons on his feet. No one was strong enough to subdue him" (Mark 5:2–4).

Wrong. No one, except Jesus. The Bible tells us that Jesus confronted the evil spirit in this wild man, and something miraculous happened—as it always does when Jesus touches a life.

As the nearby townspeople came out to see Jesus, "They saw the man who had been possessed ... sitting there, dressed and in his right mind" (Mark 5:15). What a transformation!

Obviously, you are not living in a cemetery or breaking chains or housing demons. But there may be an anger, a darkness inside you that you have not been able to control. This miracle by Jesus gives hope to all of us who battle with something in us that we cannot master. Jesus has the power to touch what is out of control and bring peace to it.

Your anger has controlled you long enough. It is time for you to begin to control your anger. Eight winning weapons can help you finally beat the anger that has beaten you for too long.

Weapon #1: Big Ears

Dumbo had them, and you need them. His big ears helped him be a flying elephant. Your big ears will not take you that high, but they will help you rise above the volcano inside you. These big ears have nothing to do with large protrusions on either side of your head. They have to do with how you listen.

God makes it clear that big ears have a lot to do with putting the brakes on your temper—"Everyone should be quick to listen, slow to speak and slow to become angry" (James 1:19). This is so simple, it's almost a no-brainer.

Listen up and you will be less likely to blow up! Simple, but not easy.

When your emotions are boiling up inside, it's easy to just let them explode. But the easy thing is also the destructive thing in terms of the damage it does. So you have to make a commitment to listen before you speak. Before you are in any more situations where your temper could flare up, choose to listen first.

Someone told me once, "We get most of our exercise jumping to conclusions." That is really true when we hear a person's opening sentences and react based on that limited information. For example, your mother says, "I want you to do the yard work today." Mt. Temper blows up, based on that one sentence—"You always do this to me! I don't have time, and you know it!"

Hold everything, volcano mouth! You did the opposite of what the Bible says to do—you were quick to speak, not slow. You were slow to listen, not quick. You were quick to anger, not slow.

When you are "quick to listen," you ask questions first—*before* you shoot. "What time does it have to be done by, Mom? Is there some of the job that can be done another day? Is there anyone who could help me? Do you mind if I tell you what I had planned so maybe we can get both things done?" You are pursuing more information before you jump down the throat of someone you love.

Chores are a relatively minor issue compared to issues where deeper feelings are involved. Those are the ones where you can really hurt someone with a fast-trigger response. But questions such as "What makes you say that?" or "What have I done to make you feel that way?"

or "How does that make you feel?" can take some of the heat out of the conversation.

Many conversations become two volcanoes erupting all over each other because neither person is listening to the other one. Often, you might not get angry if you could understand what the other person is saying and feeling. Usually, the first few sentences will not tell you that. You have to keep silent long enough to hear it all, then speak to ask clarifying questions, then respond to the whole issue, not a piece of it that you pounced on.

Yes, it is hard to listen when your heated emotions want to explode. But if you are serious about finally controlling your temper, it starts with big ears. After all, God Himself says you can slow down your anger if you speed up your listening.

A commitment to listen will help you use the second temper-taming weapon.

Weapon #2: The Cooldown Time-out

If the fire inside you is raging out of control, you have to allow some time to let the fire die down. Remember, that fire has too often burned the people around you. So before you answer in anger, it is important to take a step away first—to be "slow to speak." With that in mind, you start to practice a new discipline—not saying anything until you have taken a cooldown time-out. Take some time and some space to hose down the fire. Talk to God about it before you talk to any other person. Only then do you respond—with a lot of the heat gone that would have created scars.

Weapon #3: The Sundown Clock

Tupperware surprises. They can be one of the scary things about opening up the refrigerator—those multi-shaped plastic containers in which you can store the food you didn't finish. Good idea. Unfortunately, we do not always remember what we store. And day by day, Tuesday's meat loaf gets pushed back behind food from Wednesday, Thursday, Friday—until it disappears from view.

Oh, but that meat loaf will be back. One day you open the fridge, only to be staggered by an odor that could get your family an environmental fine. Some brave soul—usually poor Mom—digs into the fridge to find out where Stinky is. And then comes that sickening moment when she opens the lid on the Tupperware—only to find what last month's meat loaf has become. Microbiologists from around the world descend on your kitchen to try to identify this grotesque, intermediate life-form. The meat loaf was okay when it was fresh, but not dealing with it soon made it much worse to deal with later.

Just like your anger. In God's very wise words, "'In your anger, do not sin': Do not let the sun go down while you are still angry" (Ephesians 4:26). In other words, do not ever go to bed angry! Deal with the issues and the feelings while they are small. They will never be easier or smaller to deal with than they are right now.

In the old Westerns I used to watch when I was a kid, the sheriff would usually have a showdown with Mr. Gunslinger. He would look him in the eye and spit out this ultimatum: "I want you out of town by sundown." If you want to tame your temper, you have to face down your angry feelings and say, "I want you out of town by sundown!"

When you allow the sun to go down on angry feelings, they start to turn into resentment. If you wait to clean up your anger, your feelings become hard feelings, like the food on your dinner dishes when it's not washed off right away. And hard feelings are not easy to get rid of. In fact, they turn into unforgiveness and bitterness— which just throw more fuel on the fire inside that you are trying to control.

And when you do not immediately repair what anger broke, someone who is your enemy takes advantage of the delay—"And do not give the devil a foothold" (Ephesians 4:27). That warning follows right after God's command to have a sundown showdown with your anger. God seems to be saying that when there is an unfixed, unforgiving spot in your angry heart, it can easily turn into a Satan-spot inside you—a "foothold" from which he can grow all kinds of destructive feelings in your soul.

You cannot afford to let the fire smolder in you. If it smolders long, it will spread and destroy more than you ever could have imagined. Quench the fires of anger when they are small.

Weapon #4: The Memory Doctor

If you want to understand where the fires of anger often come from, you might want to try an experiment from my "Science for the Simple." First, you fill a glass of water to the halfway point. Then slowly pour in more, and more, and more—until the glass is filled to the top. Notice how much you can pour into a glass that is only half full. The next step is to pour just a few drops into the glass that is now full to the brim. What happens? Last step—get a towel and clean up the water you spilled all over when you tried to pour more into an already full glass!

The point is simple, as promised. When a glass is already full, it only takes a few drops to spill. That happens to people, too. When a person keeps spilling emotionally, it probably is not because of whatever incident—whatever drop—took him or her over the edge. People often spill out anger because their glass is already full of pain. Unresolved pain eventually turns into anger.

The seething feelings inside you may have their real roots in experiences that have filled your glass with hurt—from being abandoned by someone, abused, betrayed, neglected, or put down. Your painful memories keep filling up your emotional glass. There is no room left where you can put even small frustrations—so at the slightest provocation, you spill anger all over the people around you. Your volcano has so much lava built up that when it blows, it really blows.

So what do you do about your full glass? Obviously, you have to find a way to empty out some of those painful memories. The symptom of anger will never go away until the disease of hurt inside is dealt with. Which brings us to the Memory Doctor—someone who can begin to help the hurts that fuel the anger.

That Doctor is Jesus Christ. In fact, the Bible says that Jesus "took up our infirmities and carried our sorrows" (Isaiah 53:4). He came "to bind up the brokenhearted" (Isaiah 61:1). Jesus understands our pain. He was "a man of sorrows, and familiar with suffering" (Isaiah 53:3). But He also has divine power to go back through your past with you and begin to heal those painful memories.

It may be that you have been unwilling or afraid to face the ugly monsters of the past. But they keep surfacing anyway in the form of your often uncontrollable anger. The good news is that you can dare to confront the wounds that are the real source of the fire inside—if you have opened your life to the Savior, Jesus Christ. He offers to walk with you through those painful memories, helping you carry the load and healing the wounds.

Weapon #5: The Victim Visits

When our daughter Lisa was little, we displayed most of her artwork on the refrigerator door. We were proud of her creative efforts. Usually. There was the time my wife was painting the woodwork in Lisa's room and stopped briefly to answer the phone in another room. She gave Lisa one instruction—"Do not touch the paint." When Karen returned from her call, little Miss Rembrandt was working on a three-year-old's masterpiece. Unfortunately, she had chosen the wall for her canvas. There on her bedroom wall were "Designs by Lisa" in the paint that was intended only for the woodwork.

Mom did not spank; she did not even yell. She just went and got a bucket of water and a rag and gave Lisa a new instruction—"Clean it up." Speaking of Mission Impossible! Lisa scrubbed and scrubbed, to little avail. But she learned that we are responsible for the messes we make. By the way, that was Lisa's one and only wall painting.

As you determine that you will tame your temper, there is an important cleanup step that will help you get control. It has to do with going back to try to clean up some of the messes your anger may have created. For all of us, there are people who have been "nuked" at some time by our temper. And we need to go back to those people, apologize, and try to repair the damage we have done. It may be a parent, another family member, a friend, a former boyfriend or girlfriend, a coworker—anyone who may be carrying scars from our "reckless words" that pierced "like a sword."

A "make it right" visit with a victim of your volcano makes a difference for them and for you. For the person you have hurt, your willingness to apologize and ask forgiveness can help erase those ugly memories from the tape in their heart. For you, there is the wonderful feeling of a new beginning as you clean up the wreckage that may have damaged some relationships. And, like our daughter facing the consequences of the mess she made, your cleanup efforts will help you count the cost of your angry actions and give you reason not to make that mistake again.

Weapon #6: The Enemy Changer

If I gave you a card and asked you to write down the three people who have hurt or frustrated you the most in your life, what names would you put there? Those would be some of the people who are your enemies. Now think about those people as you read these disturbing, radical words of Jesus—"Love your enemies, do good to those who hate you, bless those who curse you, pray for those who mistreat you" (Luke 6:27–28).

Did you catch those verbs—"love," "do good to," "bless," "pray for." Doesn't that sound like the opposite of how you feel like treating the people you are angry with? But Jesus is not asking us to have gooey love feelings for those people who have given us no reason to love them. He is telling us to choose to treat them lovingly, feelings or not. The alternative is for the fires of anger to burn higher and higher, injuring not only your "enemies," but many inno- cent people around you—including you. Anger lashes out in every direction when it is allowed to smolder inside you. So you will not be able to control your temper until you flush out the strongholds of anger inside you—the ones that have the names of those "enemies" on them.

So, you need to pursue Jesus' plan for removing your enemies—by making them non-enemies. That begins as you obey Jesus' command to "pray for those who mis- treat you." Something happens when you begin to pray every day for the people you cannot stand, for the people that make you angry. For one thing, your daily prayer for God's blessing on them and for their heart may begin to change the kind of person they are. But whether or not they change, *you* will change. It is almost impossible to pray regularly for a person and still have angry feelings toward them. Prayer changes people—beginning with the person doing the praying! And as you pray, ask God for the grace to treat that person as Jesus would, to help you be a carrier of the love of Jesus Christ into their life.

When you begin to pray for and care for the people who have wounded you most, you are into Advanced Volcano Management. You are on your way to really winning the battle.

Weapon #7: The Justice Giver

Out of anger grow feelings of revenge. As long as you hang onto those feelings, your volcano will continue to blow. God has a better idea: "Do not repay anyone evil for evil.... If it is possible, as far as it depends on you, live at peace with everyone. Do not take revenge, my friends, but leave room for God's wrath, for it is written: 'It is mine to avenge; I will repay,' says the Lord" (Romans 12:17–19).

So you smolder inside, grumbling, "What that person did to me just isn't right! Somebody should give him what he has coming!" And God answers, "I agree. Leave it to Me." It is not your job to "get even" or punish a person who may have wronged you. That is God's job—and He will do a much better job of it than you ever could. When we try to "repay evil for evil," we interfere with the perfect justice the Ultimate Judge plans to carry out. None of us has the right to put on the Judge's robes and dispense justice to anyone else. When you try to be a vigilante and take justice into your own hands, you just mess up the better repaying God will do.

Besides, those revenge feelings keep feeding the temper you want to tame. They keep stirring up the very dark emotions you are trying to control. When you release "giving that person what he/she deserves" to God, you deprive your anger of a major fuel supply. And the fire starts to go down. When you hang onto those "get even" feelings, you just create more problems. There is a wonderful new freedom when you let go of those feelings and choose to trust the guaranteed, always perfect justice of God.

Weapon #8: Jesus-Glasses

Jesus had this amazing ability to see beyond a person's outside to what was inside making that person tick. Because of that ability, He could treat them differently than others who only saw a person's hardness or hurtful behavior. When Jesus met a woman who everyone else saw as a hard and immoral woman (John 4), He saw a woman whose spiritual emptiness had driven her to one bad relationship after another—and He changed her life. Even when He looked at the people who had just nailed Him to a cross, He saw people who did not know what they were doing. So instead of asking God to destroy them, He was able to ask God to forgive them (Luke 23:34).

"Jesus-glasses" enable you to see people in a way you could never see them before—especially the people who have hurt you. He can help set you free from anger by giving "eyes" to see beyond that person's hostile deeds to the needs inside them that make them act that way.

Hostile people are usually hurting people—people who never conquered the anger inside them and who are now spilling their anger on you. Frankly, that could be you in a few years if you do not start taming your temper now. It will help you treat that person more gently if you can see them as a hurtee, not just a hurter—a person who has been wounded along the way and needs compassion, not more wounding.

Dr. Jesus is the "eye doctor" who gives you the ability to see the people in your world as He sees them. When you ask Him for that new outlook, He can help you actually become part of the healing of that person with whom you have been so angry—by bringing some love and forgiveness into the life of a wounded, angry person. And, in so doing, you can keep yourself from becoming a person just like that.

Scary X-rays

My wife Karen and I have had a very long honeymoon. It started on our wedding day, and it is still going on over thirty years later! Our "honeymoon" was in its early years when we got the scary news. Karen might have a very serious disease.

She had gone to get a routine physical for a new job. But when the chest X-rays came back, they were not routine—they showed suspicious dark spots on her lungs. That usually means tuberculosis. The honeymooners were hurting all of a sudden. We got that report on a Friday, and the doctor said he would not have the final analysis until Monday. Welcome to the longest weekend of our lives, waiting out news that could radically change our lives.

Strangely, when the doctor met with Karen on Monday, he wanted to talk about chickens, and farms, and chicken houses, and growing up in the Midwest. He asked my wife if those things had been a part of her childhood. They had—and they helped explain those scary dark spots. As it turned out, they were evidence of a mild illness Karen had as a child—that the doctor now identified as something called histoplasmosis. That tongue-twisting word described a disease that tends to occur in childhood, to kids who grow up on Midwestern farms where they breathe some of the bacteria left by chickens. The spots look a lot like the "fingerprints" of tuberculosis; thankfully, the spots on Karen's lungs were only the scars left over from a far less serious childhood illness. Hooray for the honeymooners!

When my father was a young man (before there was a me), he had similar X-rays. They revealed what really was tuberculosis—a disease that was life-threatening, especially then. For my dad, that discovery meant two long years in a hospital to save his life and beat that deadly disease.

An X-ray can reveal some very bad news. But facing those dark spots inside you can start the healing and even save your life.

God does heart X-rays—pictures of what is going on inside the deepest parts of you. And if He illuminated your X-ray to show you what He has found, you might very well see some deadly dark spots on your soul. "This is all that anger," He might say. "It is a very damaging disease. It hurts you. It hurts the people you love. And it is only going to get worse as time goes on. I must be honest with you—if you do not beat this, it can be deadly."

This darkness inside you is actually not the real disease. It is just an ugly symptom of the real killer disease inside you. It is a spiritually terminal condition the Bible calls sin. Sin is so much more than just the breaking of somebody's religious rules—it is actually ignoring God and taking over the control of your own life, a life God gave you and God was supposed to run.

In God's own words—"We all, like sheep, have gone astray, each of us has turned to his own way" (Isaiah 53:6). This living away from God means that people live with a two-word life motto—"My way." So when other people do not let you have your way, you blow up. When other people frustrate, disappoint, or hurt you, you erupt all over them. The "my way" monster in you just keeps throwing gasoline on the fire of anger—and the fire burns totally out of your control. This battle against the sin that darkens your soul, against the anger that scars your life, seems hopeless.

Except for that one hope word. Savior. A Savior is someone who can rescue you when you cannot rescue yourself—like a firefighter leading you out of a burning building or a lifeguard saving you from drowning. And if you are tired of the darkness of sin and anger inside, you are ready for a Savior. For *the* Savior. For Jesus.

Facing the Fury

In the summer of 1996, a mother decided to take her three children out for a scenic ride by horseback. It was a beautiful day to enjoy the mountain scenery of western Canada. With her were her two preteen children and seven-year-old Stephen. They could never have imagined the terror that awaited them on a rock ledge just ahead.

Out of nowhere, a cougar suddenly pounced on little Stephen, knocking him to the ground. As that vicious cat began to tear and claw at her son, his mother responded immediately. She leaped from her horse and began to scream and wave her arms. She was trying to draw the cat's attention away from her son and to her. It worked. In an instant, the cougar left the bleeding boy and turned all his fury on that mother. The other children gathered up Stephen and rode full speed to get help. When the help arrived, it was too late for that courageous mom. She had taken all the fury of the animal on herself and died so someone she loved wouldn't have to die.

That is what Jesus was doing for you on that brutal cross where He died. He faced your killer animal called sin—with all its anger, all its destructiveness, all its hell. He saw it tearing you apart. And He said, "Take Me instead."

When you reach for the hand of your Savior, He will hold you and never let you go. And the sin-rescue has begun.

The darkness inside you not only messes up life here on earth—it costs you eternal life. The Bible says that "your iniquities have separated you from your God" (Isaiah 59:2). But when you turn from your "my way" life to Jesus, all those dark feelings in you that sin has caused can now begin to experience the healing, transforming power of Jesus Christ. The fire that has burned inside for so long is finally under control. The volcano that has blown so many times is wonderfully and miraculously at peace.

7 The Ugliest Island in the World

TICKING TIME BOMB #7:
Choosing Loneliness Instead of Challenging Loneliness

There's a beautiful spot on the coast of Maine called Bar Harbor—because there's a bar in the harbor.

It is a sandbar that is totally exposed at low tide and totally submerged at high tide. The bar goes from the mainland to a little island called—yes, Bar Island. The island is okay, but you would not necessarily want to spend a lot of time there. But some people do—a lot more time than they planned to spend.

Our family walked across the sandbar one day at low tide and spent a little while exploring the island on the other side. The day before we had seen Bar Harbor when the tide was in—and there was no trace of the sandbar. But for a few hours between the time the tide is going out and the time it rolls back in, hello, sandbar! Hello, island walk! The Bar Islanders provide these tide tables, giving you the times the tide will be coming and going—so the tourists can know when to head back from the island.

While we were checking out the island, we made sure we kept checking out the time, too. And as we started to walk back across the sandbar, we noticed that it was not as wide as it had been when we walked over to the island. In fact, we had to walk through a little water this time—the tide was coming back. What was funny was watching some people who came a few minutes after us. They were trying to wade in ocean up to their chests, holding their cameras, their backpacks, and their kids above their heads. And some people totally missed the time when they could get back. Tourists are so intelligent. If you do not watch the time and the tide, I suppose you can end up spending an unscheduled night in the woods on Bar Island. No one has to be stranded on that island. There is a way off ... but some people do not take it.

Lonely Island is a lot like that. You will not find Lonely Island on any world map—but it is an island you have visited, maybe many times. It is an emotional island we all spend time on. You could be stranded in a lonely time even as you are reading these words—you are feeling isolated, ignored, left out, forgotten, misunderstood, or out of place. Whatever the reason, you feel pretty much alone. If you are not on Lonely Island right now, you have been, and you will be again. "Lonely" is one feeling we all know a lot about, and one that can really hurt.

What Triggers Loneliness

You can't con your mommy into another drink of water. You have run out of excuses for not going to sleep. She is leaving for good this time. And you are suddenly lying there in the dark—all alone—except for the monsters who live in your closet and only come out at night.

A little kid's dark bedroom can be a pretty scary place sometimes. And maybe it's the first place we feel that feeling that will come to haunt us thousands of times throughout our life—loneliness. From our preschool years, through our teenage years, right into our adult years, and all the way to our lonely times as we live the last of our years—there are so many experiences that leave us on Lonely Island.

We get blown to Lonely Island by a storm—some unscheduled turbulence in our life that suddenly leaves us stranded emotionally. Loneliness can be triggered by those dreaded words, "Breakup." Here was a romantic relationship that had been an emotional anchor, and in one night it is swept away by "breaking up." And it hurts.

But other kinds of relationships break, too—your relationship with a close friend, with your mom or dad, with some other important person in your life. An argument, a divorce, a misunderstanding, a betrayal—relationships are fragile and storms like these can weaken or break what once was close. Hello, Lonely Island.

What hurts even more is when you permanently lose an important person in your life. I still remember the night my parents left me alone in our Chicago apartment to go to a funeral. I was about nine years old. I was doing okay until it got to be past the time they were supposed to return—and I heard a siren wailing in the distance. It probably had something to do with the fact that they had gone to a funeral—but the siren started me thinking, *I'll bet Mom and Dad died!* They didn't, and they were home in a few more minutes. But in those minutes I struggled with the first "what if my parents die?" fears I can remember. Down deep inside, we all have fears of losing people we love and count on. Sometimes, those fears become reality, and suddenly one of those people is gone. The strong winds of death are a storm that blow our ship right into Lonely Island.

But it is not always a lost relationship that causes our lonely times—it can be a nonrelationship—with a person we need to be close to, but aren't. A lot of young people live physically close to their family, but they feel emotionally distant, emotionally detached. Home was supposed to be the one place you could retreat to people you can count on. If it is not, then it can become one of the loneliest places on earth.

For some, the nonrelationship that sends them to Lonely Island is the lack of friends or the lack of a romantic relationship. Those times of "no friends" or "not many friends" can drive you deeply into yourself and to the barren shores of Lonely Island.

The kinds of storms that drive us to Lonely Island are almost endless—going into a new situation, for example. I went to three different high schools, and I had to keep starting over socially. Standing in front of another new high school, knowing no one, gave me some of the loneliest moments of my teenage years. Failure is another storm that can make you feel pretty isolated—"I blew it, and no one wants to have anything to do with me." Being talked about behind your back, feeling as if no one understands—the list of storms that leave us lonely goes on and on.

But it is not always the storm's fault that we end up on Lonely Island. Sometimes we send ourselves there. By going into hiding, for example. If you go and hide out in your room or music or some other "cave," you are cutting yourself off from other people. Or you can just shut down emotionally, treating everyone as if you have hung a "closed" sign around your neck. That kind of reaction sends "stay away" signals to the people around you—and they probably will. And you will get a free ticket to Lonely Island.

Self-pity is another attitude that can send you into isolation. When you spend most of your time complaining and feeling sorry about yourself, most people will start backing away—they don't need your negative attitude. A lot of times we blame other people for not being there when it is actually our negative or selfish attitude that drove them away.

Whether a life-storm blows us to Lonely Island or we send ourselves there with our attitude, the feelings of abandonment and isolation can be devastating. But if someone comes knocking at your door and says, "I'm here to introduce you to the new 'No More Lonely' pill," close the door. Loneliness is a fact of life.

We need people. God created us that way. Beginning with the very first human being, Adam, God said, "It is not good for the man to be alone" (Genesis 2:18). The problem is that people are going to let us down—they will not always be there for you. And life is going to keep changing, which means losing and gaining relationships. So loneliness is here to stay—but you don't have to stay lonely!

You do not usually get to choose whether you *go* to Lonely Island ... but you can choose whether or not you *stay*. Which leads us to the surprising secret about loneliness—staying lonely is not a prison sentence, it is a choice! You may get blown to Lonely Island, but you can get off that island quickly—if you make the right choices.

The Danger Zone

Loneliness can be a lot like those fun house mirrors— the ones that make you look totally distorted. When you are feeling isolated and cut off, things can look pretty distorted to you. And you can make some damaging decisions. You are vulnerable when you are lonely—and you can easily make some major mistakes. To be blunt, lonely people can make some really dumb choices. They want relief. But they get regrets.

For example, many young people have made a sexual mistake during a lonely time, thinking that physical intimacy with someone might get them off Lonely Island. Unfortunately, they often end up feeling used, guilty, and even more isolated. Lonely times are also times when some people end up getting hooked on some pain reliever they used to feel better for a little while. People who feel alone can wander into pornography or masturbation for company or into alcohol or drugs for relief. They want an escape. They get a prison instead—the prison of a habit that has them hooked.

I have had a lot of people pour out their pain to me about a bad relationship they have gotten into—some of them with a "till death do us part" commitment. And in most of those cases, it was loneliness that distorted their judgment and made this man or woman look better than they were. Lonely people can easily run for refuge into a relationship that ends up making them more lonely than they ever were alone. Or a lonely time can drive you the other way—into yourself. In the twisted mirror of lone-liness, it can look as if the whole world is against you and the situation is hopeless—so you just withdraw into a cave where nobody can hurt you or love you. You sentence yourself to a life without love.

Lonely Island is not like Bar Island in Maine where you can get stranded by high tide. It's pretty safe if you happen to get stranded there. But Lonely Island is a dangerous place. If you stay there very long, you are likely to stumble into one of the many pits or traps there. When you end up on Lonely Island—no matter what got you there—you have to get off fast! When you don't, you detonate one of those damaging time bombs—*choosing* loneliness instead of *challenging* loneliness.

Yes, you can challenge loneliness. You do not just have to sit there in a corner by yourself and sigh, "I'm just lonely, and there's nothing I can do about it." There *is* something you can do about it. Remember, staying lonely is a choice. And there are four positive choices you can make that will always be your ticket off Lonely Island.

Choice #1: I Will Find Someone Who Needs Me

There's a ride at Disney World called "Small World." You climb inside a little boat and start moving slowly into a brightly lit tunnel. On every side, you are surrounded by singing dolls, looking like children from all over the world—Japanese children in their kimonos, Eskimo children in their parkas, Mexican children with their sombreros, American children eating pizza—well, you get the idea. And the kids are all singing this adorable little song—"It's a small world after all ... it's a small world after all ... it's a small world after all ... it's a small, small world." "It sounds a little repetitious," you say. A little? They just keep repeating it and repeating it and repeating it. No matter how many bends you round on the river, no matter how many cultures you cross in that tunnel, the song just keeps playing. There's no escape. You start mumbling, "If I hear that song one more time ..."—and you hear it forty-two more times! That night you wake up in the middle of a nightmare where you are being chased by little dolls singing "It's a small world after all."

It is a frustrating thing to be trapped in a "small, small world." Unfortunately, that is exactly what happens to many of us when we hit a lonely time. We get stuck in that "small, small world" where we become focused on ourselves. "Lonely me ... poor me ... hurting me ... mistreated me"—does there seem to be a word that keeps showing up here? When "lonely" makes us into a me-centered person, we guarantee ourselves a long and miserable stay on Lonely Island. A world that is only as big as "me" is a world too small to live in.

So, at a time when your loneliness leaves you thinking a lot about yourself, it is important to decide to look beyond yourself. The less you feel like reaching out to the needs of others, the more important it is for you to do it. Instead of sitting around waiting for someone to meet your needs, you dust yourself off and ask, "Who needs me right now? Who can I be a help to? An encouragement to?" No, you do not feel like reaching out when you are feeling lonely, but remember—reaching out is not a feeling, it's a choice. And it's a choice that will rescue you from Lonely Island.

It happened to Megan. She was involved in my Campus Life group—and one of the most depressed girls I knew. A lot of that had to do with her loneliness. Megan was a bright girl with a lot of potential, but she spent a lot of time alone. She was self-conscious because she was a little overweight, and she had never had a date. Plus things at home weren't the greatest. So I often got several calls a week from Megan—to talk about her problems. She was sentencing herself to a small world by focusing so much on herself. Because of that, she compounded her loneliness by not being much fun to be around.

During one of her "I'm depressed" calls to me, I told her something that shocked her at first—"I don't want you to call me at all next week." For a moment, she probably thought even I was rejecting her. But I explained that I wanted her to try an "escape from Lonely Island" experiment instead of just talking more about the same problems. "Megan, I want you to go over to this senior citizens' home and volunteer to help some night next week." She was hesitant at first, but she agreed to do it.

Well, the night she volunteered, Megan was a hit! She visited with some of those lonely older people, listened to their stories, read to them, encouraged them. But guess who got the most encouraged? Megan! As she was leaving, several seniors asked her when she would be back. Actually, Megan came back the next week, the week after that, and the week after that. In fact, she became an angel of mercy in those people's lives twice a week from then on until she went to college. And she didn't call much anymore to talk about how lonely she was—she was too busy being the answer for other people's loneliness. The last I knew, Megan had gone on to become a doctor—making a life out of helping people.

Megan experienced the truth of a world-enlarging statement from God: "He who refreshes others will himself be refreshed" (Proverbs 11:25). That kind of "refreshing others" can be your ticket off the island and out of your lonely time.

One good way to think of some people who need someone like you is to fill in the blank in this sentence: Some of the lonely people where I live are people who

_____.

Your answers might include people who "are in the hospital," "are senior citizens who don't have much company," "are new in town and don't know anybody," "are sick with disease or handicapped," "just had their parents split up," "just had someone they love die"—you can make a pretty long list if you take a few minutes to think about the lonely people. You might even conclude that a member of your own family is going through a lonely time right now. The question is, "Will you do something to make a difference in someone else's life?" You know what "lonely" feels like—so you know how to encourage someone who is lonely.

So don't camp out on Lonely Island. Make yourself leave the island to find someone who needs you.

Choice #2: I Will Explore a Larger World

One reason we stay in the small world of loneliness is because we do not move out to explore some areas beyond what we already know. This is an exciting world, with millions of opportunities and experiences to explore.

So, there is no excuse for being holed up in your room or with a handful of people.

One good way to use your time alone and not just be alone is to expand your interests. Instead of just "blobbing out," explore some new music. Work on getting your room and your life organized. Build some relationships and provide some encouragement by using alone time to write to people. Try putting your feelings into poetry or write them down in a journal. Read some positive material. Work on developing a new skill (mechanical, musical, cooking, artistic, athletic). But you cannot afford to wallow in your lonely time. You need to *capture* your lonely time.

I watched my son Doug go through a painfully lonely time when a knee injury suddenly ended his high school football career. Football had practically been his life since he entered high school—his free time, his friends, his identity were all wrapped up in his sport. And then, in one painful moment on the field, all that was gone. As his friends continued their busy life of games and practices, Doug sat at home. As they talked about their football world, Doug was suddenly an outsider.

He went to Lonely Island—but he did not stay there. He decided to explore a larger world. He chose the world of music. Doug got a rhythm guitar and began to teach himself how to play it. As the years have unfolded, Doug has become a gifted writer of contemporary Christian music and the leader of an exciting band that is reaching out to young Native Americans. He escaped from loneliness by taking the risk of expanding his interests. So can you.

Another way to enlarge your world is to expand your friendships. The old saying warns us not to "put all your eggs in one basket." A lot of young people make the "one basket" mistake when it comes to friends. They hang everything on one or two friends. If something happens to those friends—hello, Lonely Island. Obviously, the risks of ending up alone are not as great if you develop a bigger circle of friends.

When you don't do that, you tend to smother the one or two friends you have. Since they are your peer world, you try to get them to be everything for you. And many times that leads to losing a friendship because you squeeze that friend too tightly.

When you have a small friendship world, you tend to demand too much of the few people in that world. You can counterattack against loneliness, though, by taking the initiative to enlarge your circle of friends. You might say, "That's risky. I don't feel like trying to make more friends." Again, doing what it takes to lose your loneliness is not a feeling—it's a choice. You have to make a decision that you will go places and do things that will give you a bigger social circle. That might mean getting involved in a school activity, in a youth group, in going on a missions trip where people tend to get real close, real fast.

The point is that you break out of your small circle of friends. When you do, you reduce the likelihood of ever being totally isolated or totally disappointed. If one friend is all you have—and that one friend lets you down—you are suddenly island-bound. But if you have many friends, preferably from more than one group, you almost always have somewhere to turn.

The choice to enlarge your world—through expanded interests and expanded friendships—is a strong insurance policy against being stuck on Lonely Island.

Choice #3: I Will Repair the Broken Connections

It is obvious what to do when a bone is broken—get it fixed. It should be obvious what to do when a relationship is broken—get it fixed.

One cause of a chronic lonely feeling inside you may be a relationship that is broken—and you have left it broken. Because that person is "missing" in your life, there is this cold, lonely place in your heart. It will not go away until that relationship is fixed. So the choice for you is to say, "I will do everything within my power to deal with what caused the break and fix this relationship." That may mean saying "I'm sorry" or "I forgive you" or "Please forgive me." And even though that humbling kind of initiative is not something you feel like doing, you choose to do it. The alternative is feelings that turn harder and harder and a lonely spot inside you that gets bigger and bigger.

If we had left my son's arm broken—maybe because it would hurt to get it fixed—the result would have been greater pain and lifelong limitations. Refusing to repair a broken relationship—maybe because it will hurt to get it fixed—can have the same crippling effect on you. It has already stranded you on Lonely Island long enough.

Choice #4: I Will Depend on One Anchor Relationship

Four little cards. You would not believe what stress they caused a roomful of teenagers.

It was a meeting where I gave every teenager four index cards and a pencil. I asked them to write on those cards the four most important things in their life, one on each card. It might be a person, a possession, an activity, an ability—whatever was really important to them.

When they finished writing on their cards, the stress began. I asked them to make a choice. "A disaster has just hit your life," I told them, "and you will lose one of the four most important things in your life. But unlike real life, you get to choose which one. Drop that card on the floor." There was a little buzz and then some brief frowns, but everyone managed to decide which treasure they would drop.

It got a little more tense when I told them that "another disaster comes along, and you again have to lose something or someone important to you. Which one will it be? Drop that card on the floor." Suddenly, these were definitely not happy campers. But after a little hesitation, a second card fell to the ground.

I almost caused a walkout when I said, "Once more, circumstances beyond your control are going to cost you one of the most important things in your life. You can keep one—but the other one has to go." Almost everybody looked at me with that "get real, Ron" look. Some said they either would not or could not drop one of those last two cards. But eventually every person struggled through that painful choice and dropped the second-to-the-last card.

Then I said, "You are now holding in your hand the most important thing in your life. I have just one question about it—one to which I don't need an answer, but you do. Here's the question about your most important thing: Is it something you can lose? If the answer is yes, then you have to live your whole life knowing that you may lose it."

I will never forget the night I held my last two "cards" in my hand. My wife Karen had a critical case of hepatitis—critical enough that she might not make it. On a night when the disease was ravaging her body, she began to talk as I have never heard her talk before—like people talk when they feel they're dying. I knew that Karen and I would never choose to leave each other, but this night the choice was out of our hands. I dropped to my knees next to her bed and begged God to spare her life. And I am forever grateful to Him that He did.

What if this had been God's time for her to leave? What if I had my card that says "Karen" taken from my hand that night? The honest answer is—it would have left a gaping hole in my life. But I would have still had one card left. My last card—my most important thing— is my personal relationship with Jesus Christ. And here is His awesome promise to anyone who belongs to Him—"Never will I leave you; never will I forsake you" (Hebrews 13:5).

Karen would never choose to leave me—nor would I choose to leave her. But I learned that night that we don't always get the choice. All our earth-loves are losable. You can lose a mother, father, husband, wife, or close friend— but you can't lose Jesus!

In fact, God tells us that nothing "in all creation, will be able to separate us from the love of God that is in Christ Jesus our Lord" (Romans 8:39). We need a love like that. We need an anchor relationship—one that holds us steady when everything and everyone is being blown away.

Actually, you have known you need a relationship like this for a long time—you just may not have known with whom that relationship was supposed to be. The first whisper of that need is a little voice inside you that says, "Someone's missing." We've all felt at sometime that there is something we're *supposed* to have that we *don't* have. We think it's a best friend—until we get a best friend and still feel like someone's missing. Maybe it's a lot of friends we need—but we get more friends and the loneliness is still there. Well, maybe "someone" is a boyfriend or girl-friend—again, we get that person but still have the empti-ness. Some people go their whole lives looking for that missing person—in a husband or wife, in children, in being popular. But there is always "someone missing."

Someone *is* missing, because instead of living for the One who created us, we have lived for ourselves. We have basically told God, "You run the universe—I will run me." The Bible has a word for this rebellion against our Creator—sin. Notice the middle letter is "I." Each of us has said, "*I* will run my life," with choices that go against God and His plans for us.

We are empty until we find the Someone we were made for. God makes it very clear who that is when He says about Jesus Christ, "All things were created by him and for him" (Colossians 1:16). In our Creator's own words, we were made *by* Jesus, we were made *for* Jesus, and we are going to have a hole in our heart until we *have* Jesus. Our deepest loneliness—the kind that never seems to go away no matter what other relationships we have—is actually cosmic loneliness.

What causes this cosmic loneliness? God says, "Your iniquities have separated you from your God" (Isaiah 59:2). To put it another way, your sins have built a mas-sive wall between you and God. You probably have felt that wall between you—it cuts you off from the greatest love in the universe. If you die with that wall still there, it is there forever. Which makes hell a place of utter and irreversible loneliness.

But Jesus loves you so much that He refused to leave you cut off from Him. The only way you could ever have the relationship you were made for is to have the death penalty paid for your sin. The Bible says someone paid it, "He himself [Jesus] bore our sins in his body on the tree" (1 Peter 2:24). On the cross where He paid for your sins, He endured the loneliest moment in history, crying out in agony, "My God, my God, why have you forsaken me?" (Matthew 27:46). Here was the one and only Son of God—who had never had one moment in all eternity when His relationship with His Father was broken—suddenly abandoned by God. Why? Because He was carrying all your sin and mine—and God cannot have anything to do with sin.

You did the sinning. Jesus did the dying. And because of that, the deepest loneliness in your heart can finally be cured. Now this Jesus waits to tear down the wall that has separated you from your Creator. This ultimate relationship begins the moment you put your trust in Him. If you remain cosmically lonely, it will be because you choose to deny His love for you. God's Book says, "God so loved the world that he gave his one and only Son, that whoever believes in him shall not perish but have eternal life" (John 3:16). God loves you, but if you choose to ignore or reject Jesus, you are choosing ultimate loneliness forever.

You can stop the loneliness by believing in God and His love for you. "Believe" means total trust, total commitment. Your personal relationship with Jesus Christ begins when you say to Him, "Lord, I have been running my life. I resign. I realize that I was made by You and for You, and I've lived for me. I know that's a sin, which has a death penalty. I believe when You died on the cross, You were paying for my sins. You are my only hope of removing the wall between God and me, of ever going to heaven, of ever having a relationship with God. I'm putting all my trust in You, Lord, and want to begin my personal relationship with You today." If you prayed that prayer, your anchor relationship has just begun.

You will have your share of lonely times in the months and years ahead. And there are choices you can make that will help your stay on Lonely Island be a short one—finding someone who needs you, exploring a larger world, repairing the broken connections.

But no choice you will ever make will be more life-changing than the one to depend on an anchor relationship—your relationship with Jesus Christ. If you tell Jesus you want to belong to Him, then nothing "in all creation, will be able to separate us from the love of God that is in Christ Jesus our Lord" (Romans 8:39).

In other words, you have just spent your last day alone.

8 The Tomorrow Robber

TICKING TIME BOMB #8:

Getting Desperate Enough to Give Up Your Tomorrows

will never be nominated for a Grammy award. I might be nominated for a Dummy award, though.

My associate Rick and I had just finished up a youth event in Canada and returned to our hotel rooms. Just before he went to his room he handed me an envelope, folded in half, with a phone number written on it. He told me to call a family member at that number. Later, as I was packing to leave, I threw away all the junk I had accumulated over the weekend, including that envelope with the telephone number. I had returned the call, and I did not need the number anymore.

When we got back home, I asked Rick, "Did they give you the check to cover our travel expenses?" Wrinkling his brow, Rick said, "I gave that to you. Remember?" I didn't. "It was in that envelope with the phone number on it." Uh ... oh. Somehow, either he had forgotten to tell me, or I had been too busy to hear it, but the fact remained—I had just discarded something pretty valuable—in a hotel trash can in another country. Nice work! Thankfully, our Canadian hosts—understanding the I.Q.

they were dealing with—were gracious enough to reissue that check. Of course, when I was tossing that envelope, I had no idea of the value of what I was throwing away.

Day after day, young people are making that same mistake, only with the most valuable possession they have ever been given—their life. A young man or young woman is deciding to die. Another teenage suicide. And the One who created that young person must say with tears in His eyes, "How could she just throw away what was worth so much?"

And God isn't the only one who cries. Recently, I returned home late one night and played back the messages that had been left on our answering machine. The first message was from Angie, a young friend of ours. She was choking back tears as she blurted out her pain in one sentence: "My friend across the street committed suicide last night." It was just like every suicide—those who loved the one who killed herself were left to cry some of the most bitter tears a human being can cry.

We cannot confront life's ticking time bombs without facing the one that, in many ways, is the most devastating of all. It is the one mistake that is forever irreversible—getting desperate enough to give up your tomorrows.

Tragically, thoughts of self-destruction are part of more young people's lives than ever before. One report tells us that one out of three young people has thought about killing themselves—and one out of seven has actually tried to end their life. Something is very wrong in this picture. At a time when a young person should be thinking about making a future, too many are deciding not to have one.

And it does not always take even a major tragedy to drive a teenager over the edge. When Cara told me about the night she overdosed on pills and almost died, I was surprised at how she answered my question, "Why?" "Because," she explained, "my boyfriend was mean to me at school that day ... and then I had an argument with my parents when I got home." Cara had a bad day—but bad enough to throw away the rest of her life?

The national news reported on a fourteen-year-old boyfriend and girlfriend whose parents did not approve of their relationship and forbade them from seeing each other. Their response? They walked to a nearby bridge and jumped to their deaths together. No doubt it hurt to have their young romance broken up—but enough to trash the next sixty years of their lives?

Many young people would say, "I would never do anything like that." And many wouldn't. But there are some—maybe you, or someone you know—who, if the pain got intense enough, might think about checking out of life as one of their options. While the reasons may look small to other people, those reasons can feel very big to you when you are hurting. And the reasons may relate to some genuinely major life-tragedy. But suicide is never the right answer. Because suicide is the "tomorrow rob-ber"—it robs you of all your tomorrows. And no pain is so great that it's worth the awful price of ending your own life.

You may be reading this, knowing that there are times when the dark feelings inside you are pretty strong—maybe almost overwhelming. The hurt is real, the issues are painful, and the desire for the pain to stop can be very intense. That is when the unthinkable may start to become thinkable to you.

But this is not time to let desperation win. It is a time for hope. And there is a lot of hope in these next few pages. You may need that hope right now, you may need it some time in the future when you are feeling really down, or someone you know might need it. Whatever the situation, the hope is larger than the hurt. Your tomorrows are worth sticking around for. And you are worth too much to throw away.

Too Close to the Edge

However big you expect the Grand Canyon to be, it's bigger. The first time you see it, you are amazed at how far that beautiful canyon goes. There is no one place you can stand and see all of the Grand Canyon—you just keep driving and driving, stopping at overlooks where you can see a small part of the whole thing. And each of those parts could be named the Grand Canyon by itself!

Our family has been there, and it is an awesome sight. We stopped several places and looked over—it was a very impressive view. Our big problem at the Grand Canyon is when our sons think they are part mountain goat. Of course, mountain goats cannot read the signs that tell you to stay behind the fences. Apparently, our boys can't either. They have this almost irresistible desire to forget the fence and venture out as far as possible on those rocks that overlook the canyon. Of course, one false step and you can become part of the scenery down in the canyon.

That is something Mom thinks would be a bad way to remember our vacation. So her feelings about exploring the edge have always been communicated clearly—*very* clearly. Any danger the canyon might pose pales in comparison with the danger Mom poses if you go near the edge. These discussions are held before we ever get out of the car—and the door does not open until our sons have signed a fourteen-page legal agreement that they will not shorten their mother's life by going where their lives could be shortened.

All the talk about going too far for safety's sake made a lot more sense the morning after we had stopped at that one particular overlook. Reading that morning's newspaper, I discovered that the same afternoon we had been there, two young men had gone to that same overlook, and one never came back. He ended up dead at the bottom of the canyon. All because he had stepped too close to the edge.

That is where many young people end up when life hurts—too close to the edge. And every day another young person goes over the edge, not because of an accident, but because of a decision to die. For some, it is a sudden, impulsive choice. For others, it is a "last straw" response to an accumulation of problems. For still others, it is a final act that has been considered secretly over a period of time.

While suicide is, in many ways, the biggest mistake of all, it is usually the result of some other mistakes that lead up to it. There are four wrong ideas that end up pushing a young person to the fatal edge.

A Deadly Wrong Idea—Being Wrong About Your Value

When someone is considering suicide, they are considering throwing away something very valuable—probably not realizing the worth of the person they are about to trash.

You might respond, "Well, I've been treated like trash!" I treated that envelope with the check in it like trash, too—but that did not mean it *was* trash. I just did not realize how valuable it was. If I had, I would never have even considered throwing it away. You may have been rejected, ignored, victimized, belittled—but those people who treated you that way don't know who you really are. Because of how you have been treated, you also may not realize who you are and what you are worth. Because if you did, you would never consider throwing yourself away in an act of self-destruction.

Your Creator is the only Person who can tell you who you really are and how valuable you are. He says, "We are God's workmanship, created in Christ Jesus to do good works, which God prepared in advance for us to do" (Ephesians 2:10). You are a handmade, one-of-a-kind masterpiece creation of God Himself! You are "workmanship," just like a gifted artist's priceless painting or the original work of a master craftsman. Except you were crafted by the Master Craftsman. And you are worth too much to trash.

If you are not convinced of what you are worth, then take a mental walk up the hill where Jesus Christ was dying on that cross ... where you were, in God's words, "bought at a price" (1 Corinthians 6:20). The price paid to rescue you from your sin is spelled out for you in these words, addressed to Jesus—"With your blood you purchased men for God" (Revelation 5:9).

God thought you were worth the life of His one and only Son. As you stand at the foot of Jesus' cross and look at Him pouring out His life for you, you see how much God loves you and how much He was willing to pay to get you back.

You are God's handmade, high-priced treasure ... much too valuable to throw away. It is an awful mistake to trash the life that Jesus paid so much to save.

A Deadly Wrong Idea—Being Wrong About Your Future

"And they lived happily ever after." It's a nice ending for a fairy tale, but real life is not all "happily ever afters."

When you're depressed, you may feel as if your life is going to turn out like a fairy tale in reverse—"and they lived unhappily ever after." Well, that isn't a realistic ending either!

"My future is just going to be more of the present—and the present hurts!" This "nothing is ever going to change" attitude can take you to the edge where you feel as if there is no reason to stick around. But at times like that, it is important to remember those four little letters—T.T.S.P. "This too shall pass." This is true of most difficult times in your life—they will pass. Which means that whatever is getting you down right now will probably be only temporary. If you have ever been to the hair stylist and gotten a perm, then you know even a perm lasts only about three months. Even a "perm" is a "temp."

Tragically, many young people have had the wrong idea that the problems of the present will ruin their entire future. In reality, most problems are temporary problems. But suicide is a permanent mistake.

Imagine, for example, that you are traveling on a plane, and suddenly your flight hits a stretch of bad weather.

Your plane is doing its impression of a rodeo horse, bucking all over the place. And your stomach is doing its impression of a cement mixer. To make it worse, Albert, the man in the seat next to you, is yelling, "This is awful! I hate this!" The flight attendant comes over the loudspeaker in a comforting voice and says, "Ladies and gentlemen, the captain has turned on the 'fasten seat belts' sign—please be sure you are securely seated. We are passing through a little storm system here, but we should be through this in a few minutes. Until then, sorry—no more peanuts."

After a couple more minutes of rock and roll, Albert screams, "That's it! I can't take it anymore!" He takes off his seat belt and proceeds to start weaving up the aisle. After falling into two or three laps, he finally stumbles to his goal—the nearest exit door. As he reaches for the handle, a flight attendant comes charging down the aisle like Wonder Woman. "What are you doing?" she screams to Albert. Tightening his grip on the door handle, your nutty neighbor responds, "I can't stand this storm anymore. I'm leaving." "It's 30,000 feet down!" the flight attendant yells—as she goes airborne to tackle her passenger, wildly swinging a tray. It connects. Albert slumps to the floor. Nobody messes with a flight attendant.

Of course, you do not jump out of a plane just because you are going through a storm. Storms are temporary. Jumping is forever. Unfortunately, too many young people have forgotten that when they were in the middle of a storm—and they have jumped. And lost all their tomorrows.

If you are looking for a reason to have hope for your future, you can find it in the "big picture" promise of your

Creator—"'I know the plans I have for you,' declares the LORD, 'plans to prosper you and not to harm you, plans to give you hope and a future'" (Jeremiah 29:11). God has exciting plans for your future. If you drop out early, you will miss the plans you were made for and the lives you were put here to touch. Remember, you are God's workmanship, "created to do good works which God prepared in advance" for you to do.

Your future is supposed to be a "Make A Difference" future. The only way you will miss it is if you make an exit instead. The pain of the present will eventually pass, and the plans of God are worth sticking around for.

A Deadly Wrong Idea—Being Wrong About Your Pain

When little kids play, they sometimes get banged up. When our kids would take a chunk out of a knee or an elbow, they would sometimes come running in the house to call 911—Mother. And Karen would break out the "boo-boo" kit. In our family, a "boo-boo" was the technical medical term for a wound, especially one inflicted by a nasty sidewalk or street. Out came the iodine and the Band-Aids—along with Mom's special medicine. "Here, let me kiss your boo-boo." It still amazes me and baffles the scientific world how much better a kiss can make a boo-boo feel.

But life's deepest wounds are not on your elbow or your knee—they are usually deep inside. And sometimes you are hurting so badly inside that you are sure there is no one to "kiss" a wound like this one. Your depression starts to feel unbearable when you conclude, "I'm all alone in my pain. No one can understand what I'm feeling. I have to carry this all alone."

Those feelings are true only if you choose to leave it that way. There are people who care. There are people who are even trained to help you face this monster—who have helped others face it and win. The only reason you do not experience caring during your depressing time is because you will not seek out someone who cares or let those around you care for you. If you suffer secretly, you are making it impossible for anyone to reach out to your pain. And if you do not look for a counselor or pastor or other trained helper, you are missing the very kind of person who could understand and share the load.

A depressed person might say, "I'm scared to tell anybody about this." What you should be scared of is committing suicide, not seeking help! And if it takes a little effort to seek out a trained helper, it is a small effort to make when something as valuable as your life is involved. Considering suicide without talking to someone who could help is like having problems with your car—and driving it over a cliff without ever talking to a mechanic.

Your first line of helping people is your parents. Beyond them are school counselors, pastors, therapists, telephone hotlines—there is no reason for you to carry a heavy load alone when help is, at most, a couple of phone calls away. And there is always One who is there and who understands what you're going through—Jesus. He has walked in our shoes.

When you are feeling wounded, do not withdraw from people—*seek out* people who can help share your load and give you perspective. Your greatest enemy may not be your pain—but your *silence* about your pain.

Our grown-up, inner "boo-boos" are too deep to be comforted just by a mommy's kiss. But there are people around you who are willing to "kiss" your hurt with their love, their understanding, their encouragement, and their perspective.

And when you run to Jesus with your wound, He will know exactly how you feel. He became one of us and suffered more than any of us. Jesus' arms are wide open, asking you to dump your burdens on Him—every day. He invites you to "cast all your anxiety on him because he cares for you" (1 Peter 5:7).

You do not have to be alone in your pain. Help is only a prayer or phone call away.

A Deadly Wrong Idea—Being Wrong About the Source

When you are considering taking your own life, you seldom stop to think about where this ugly idea is coming from. You need to think about it! With some revealing help from Jesus Christ. "The thief comes only to steal and kill and destroy; I have come that they may have life, and have it to the full" (John 10:10).

The "thief" Jesus talked about was none other than your eternal enemy, the devil. His goal is to somehow "steal," "kill," or "destroy" you. And what greater slap in your Creator's face than for you to destroy yourself, His deeply loved creation.

You may think that the source of suicidal feelings is your situation. Wrong. I have even had people suggest that maybe God is prompting them to end their life. Never! Ultimately, the idea of ending your own life comes from Satan himself. The voice inside you that whispers,

"You might as well give up ... you might as well die ... if you die, you'll stop hurting"—that voice is the destroyer! He tries to use your hard times and your hurting feelings to push you to an edge where you would normally never consider going. And when you "jump," you hand Satan the greatest victory he could ever win in your life.

The devil is the life-taker, and suicide is his ultimate triumph in a human life. But Jesus, on the other hand, is the life-giver. As you struggle with the dark feelings of depression and the thoughts of suicide, it is important to remember that they are coming straight from the prince of darkness, who wants you with him in hell forever. But your pain does not have to take you to the edge of death. It can take you instead to the beginning of life inside the healing love of Jesus Christ. He died so you can live.

"Word Just In . . . 'Suicide Died Today'"

Living is always better!

No matter how insurmountable the problems feel, no matter how difficult the future looks—when it comes to suicide, living is always a better choice. Why?

Suicide Is the Ultimate Defiance Toward the God Who Made You

The Bible makes it clear who is supposed to decide when and how you die. As King David speaks to God about his beginning and his ending, he says, "You created my inmost being; you knit me together in my mother's womb.... All the days ordained for me were written in your book before one of them came to be" (Psalm 139:13, 16). God decided the number of your days before you were even born. Only the One who gave you your life has the right to take it. When people rip that right from God's hand with suicide, they are committing an ultimate act of defiance before their Creator ... in the last moment before they meet Him face-to-face.

Suicide Is the Ultimate Act of Selfishness Toward the People Who Love You

I have been there with the family and the friends after someone they love has just destroyed themselves. I cannot describe the deep, gut-wrenching anguish of those dear people. Their loved one decided that the hurt was so bad that he or she would just "leave" forever—leaving behind the very people who loved them, who would bleed the rest of their lives from the wound of this tragic act.

There is no more selfish act a human being can do than suicide. It is the emotional homicide of the dearest people in your world.

Suicide Is the Ultimate Waste of the Life That Has Been Trusted to You

God put you here to make a difference. You abort all you were put here for when you quit on life. And life is such a precious gift to throw away. In hospitals all over the world right now, there are medical teams working around the clock and huge expenses being incurred just so one person can have a few more days of life. In the meantime, a depressed person somewhere decides to just throw away all the rest of their days in one ugly act of suicide. It is the ultimate waste and the ultimate surrender to the devil who hates you.

Only One Choice

When you consider the awful price tag for suicide, there seems to be only one choice—life!

In fact, that is exactly the choice your Creator is calling you to make. "Now choose life, so that you and your children may live and that you may love the LORD your God, listen to his voice, and hold fast to him. For the LORD is your life" (Deuteronomy 30:19–20).

God commands us to choose life—for three reasons.

- Because of your future children (who will never have the chance to live if you choose to die)
- Because of your relationship with God
- Because of God's plans for you

God wants you to have all the tomorrows you were created for. So you need to decide once and for all that you will be here for all those tomorrows. That life-choice starts when you nail shut the door marked "suicide." Choosing life means eliminating the death-choice. You can commit this very day to live your life from now on as if suicide is a non-option for you—no matter how bad you are hurting.

Three Life-Changing Words

The storm was winning big time.

Storms weren't anything new. Peter and Andrew had spent their lives on this lake. Fishermen like them—and their partners, James and John—had seen it all, they thought. But nothing like the night of the Storm They Would Never Forget.

All twelve of Jesus' disciples were on board that night as the storm started pounding them like a giant hammer. The fishermen aboard knew all the tricks of the trade—but the waves were so overwhelming and the winds so violent that nothing was working. The ship was being ripped apart and taking on water fast. Soaked and near panic, one of the men bellowed above the storm—"Somebody wake up Jesus!"

Yes, Jesus was on board, too—somehow sleeping in a sheltered corner, in spite of the storm. He had been working almost around the clock for days, responding to the needs of hundreds of hurting people who had come to Him as their last hope. Now it was His own disciples who came to Him with only one hope left.

"Jesus! Don't You care that we're about to die?" a desperate disciple screamed at the Master as He awakened to His name. No answer—except that He stood to His feet and began to make His way forward, clutching the railing for support. Then, as Jesus stepped toward the bow of the ship, Peter cried out, "Stay back, Lord! You'll be swept overboard!" Without comment, Jesus took one more step until He was as far forward as He could go, with one massive wave after another crashing over the bow and slamming into His body.

The rain and the waves were almost blinding now, and the disciples could only watch the drama in the bow through squinting eyes. At times, it looked as if Jesus had disappeared—if He had, they would have no way to rescue Him from the violence of this lake. But then, in the moments before the next mountain of water covered them, they saw Him standing drenched but tall, one hand gripping the railing, and one extended over the water.

Peter tried to pull himself forward to bring Jesus to safety—but as he got close to the Master, he heard the voice of Jesus so loudly that even the storm's fury could not drown it out. In a voice that sounded like a father boldly correcting an unruly child, Jesus boomed three words into the face of the storm ...

"Peace! Be still!"

Then, in a moment no man on that boat would ever forget—a moment they would tell about for years to come—the storm stopped. It didn't taper off or die down—it stopped—suddenly, completely. In an instant, the waves were no more ... the lake was calm ... the wind was gone.

And for a full minute or two, it was as quiet on the deck as it was around the ship. Finally, with Jesus still standing calmly in the bow, one of the men broke the silence. "What kind of man is this? Even the winds and the waves obey Him!"

From the Sea of Galilee to the day they would each die for this Savior, they would never face a storm that Jesus could not conquer.

And neither will you—if you have Jesus in your boat. There is no storm that He cannot overcome with His "Peace, be still." Including the storm that may be battering you right now. The one that has almost sunk you, maybe many times. But when you feel you are going down and the waves are about to win, do not abandon ship. Call on the Lord of the storm—the winds and the waves obey Him.

He may not calm the storm around you—but He will calm the storm inside you. With Jesus, there is no such thing as impossible ... or unbearable ... or hopeless. Since that out-of-control night on a seething lake, Jesus has spoken His "Peace, be still" to storms in millions of hurting lives—and His peace has always been greater than the storm.

The overwhelming emotions and deep darkness of depression do not ever have to win again. Not if you have Jesus—and His "Peace! Be still!"

9 Ambushes from Hell

TICKING TIME BOMB #9:
Opening Yourself Up to the Dark Side of the
Supernatural

It doesn't take long to make a car disappear.

No, this is not about great magic tricks. But it is about a man who made our car vanish in about sixty seconds.

When I was nine years old, one night my dad dropped off my mom and me in front of our apartment in Chicago. Snow was falling, so Dad was trying to save us the walk from the nearby garage where we parked our car. But before he could park, Mom signaled him that there was someone on the phone for him. That was all I knew until Dad went out to park the car and found no car to park. He came running back in, looking as white as the falling snow—"The car's gone!" he told us in disbelief.

When Dad ran in for that phone call, he left the keys in the ignition, knowing he would be right back. But as he thought about it later, Dad vaguely remembered seeing a man coming down the sidewalk as Dad ran inside. The tracks in the snow told the story—footprints coming down the sidewalk until they stopped in front of our apartment and turned toward where the car had been. On the spur of the moment, Mr. Snow-walker decided our car would look nice on him. Unfortunately, my Dad made it pretty easy for him—the keys were in the car, and the door was unlocked. Adios, auto!

I did not like it when somebody took our car. I really didn't like it when someone got into our apartment! It was one night when we were gone that we got burgled (if that is not a word, it should be!). I always thought we were unburglable (a form of the word that we already discussed)—no one could come in the building without having a resident let them in with a buzzer. We were on the third floor where it would be very difficult to reach a window, and the back porch door was double locked. But we still got burgled. Through the transom. The transom was like a small, rectangular "door" above the back porch door—you could leave it in the open position on hot days. This was a cold day—but my parents had made one little mistake. The front and back doors were locked, but the transom was accidentally left unlocked. Since the transom was only about 2' x 3', the thief was obviously under 400 pounds.

It was not much of an opening, but it was all he needed. Fortunately, he did not take my Captain Midnight secret decoder ring—or I would have tracked him down personally.

The car was left unlocked. The apartment was all locked up—except for one unlocked place. But in both cases, a thief got in because we left him a way to get in.

You are asking for trouble when you do that with your car, house, or life. It is more than just a burglar who is trying to find a place to get into your life—it is no one less than the most vicious terrorist in the world. And Jesus wants to show you the door or window you may have forgotten to lock.

Terrorist at Your Door

If you heard a newscast warning that terrorists were on the loose in your town, you would probably take it pretty seriously. You for sure would check all the doors and windows—maybe five or six times. You would not leave a terrorist a place to get in.

Actually, a terrorist alert has been issued by God. He refers to this dangerous intruder by the nickname that describes his approach—the lion. "Be self-controlled and alert. Your enemy the devil prowls around like a roaring lion looking for someone to devour" (1 Peter 5:8).

The devil. The terrorist of the universe. This totally evil enemy is on the loose, armed and dangerous, looking for victims. And Satan is not just God's enemy—notice that he is *your* enemy. He wants very much to break into your life, rip off everything you have that is valuable, and leave you wasted. Only God knows and tells the truth about this cosmic terrorist who wants you as his victim—He calls him "the great dragon" (Revelation 12:9) ... "the destroyer" (Revelation 9:11) ... "the evil one" (1 John 5:18) ... "a murderer from the beginning" (John 8:44) ... "the father of lies" (John 8:44) ... the one "who leads the whole world astray" (Revelation 12:9).

Obviously, Satan is real. He is powerful. He wants to destroy you because God made you. But he is no match for Jesus. In fact, "the reason the Son of God appeared was to destroy the devil's work" (1 John 3:8). If you are close to Jesus, this cosmic terrorist cannot ultimately have you because "the one who is in you [Jesus] is greater than the one who is in the world [the devil]" (1 John 4:4).

Make no mistake about it. The devil still wants to devastate your life. But he can't—unless you leave him a place to get in. Like the night our car disappeared or our apartment got burgled. We would never have opened the door and said to the thief, "Come right on in. Make yourself at home!" And you would probably never open the door to the ultimate evil of Satan—knowingly. But you might be leaving a door or window unlocked without realizing it. And that is all he needs.

The devil has to have an opening to get in. Because of that, God gives you a simple strategy for dealing with the devil—"Do not give the devil a foothold" (Ephesians 4:27). Other Bible translations say "do not give the devil an opportunity" (NASB) or a "place" (KJV). Your enemy cannot mess up your life without some cooperation—probably unwitting cooperation—from you. He simply needs an unlocked door or window to get in.

It's important to know the enemy's strategies, but remember that Jesus Christ is the One with the power. He came "to destroy the devil's work," the One who "whenever the evil spirits saw him, fell down before him and cried out, 'You are the Son of God'" (Mark 3:11).

Very few people knowingly open the door to the devil. But he has invaded millions of lives with his darkness and death—and he would like to invade yours. That is why you need to know how the devil smuggles himself into the lives of people who never meant to get involved with him. You are activating a very dangerous time bomb when you make the deadly mistake of opening yourself up to the dark side of the supernatural.

Deadly Door #1: Curiosity

For my friend Paul, the curiosity trap sprung quickly and painfully. In high school, Paul was an outstanding young leader for the Lord and an effective public communicator for Christ. Following God's calling on his life, he eventually went to seminary to learn more about God's Word.

I lost track of Paul for the next few years—until I ran into a mutual friend. I could not believe what he told me. Paul had dropped out of seminary, become an atheist, and gotten a divorce from the woman he loved. I could not imagine how this dedicated follower of Christ had fallen so far from what he once was.

Again, no news about Paul for the next few years—until he showed up at a dinner where I was speaking. We connected like long-lost brothers, just like the good old days in high school. Paul had finally come back to Jesus and to the joy and freedom he had lost during his years away. I had one burning question for my friend—"What happened?"

Paul began to tell me about a night at seminary when he needed a break from studying for final exams. He was intrigued by a blockbuster movie that had hit the theaters recently—*The Exorcist*. It was a movie that graphically portrayed demonic activity in people's lives. That night at our reunion, Paul told me, "All I know is, Ron, that something happened inside me while I was watching that movie. I can't explain it, but I only know that some kind of evil was planted in me that night—and it just took over."

I am so grateful that God rescued Paul. But he would tell you today that there are irreversible mistakes he made in his time away from God—and the scars that go with them. If someone had tried to tell him that a movie could suck his life into Satan's black hole, he never would have bought it. But that is exactly what happened.

Satan knows that a powerful portrayal of the dark side of the supernatural is all the hook he needs to capture certain hearts. It may not be one movie, or one TV show, or one occult book, or one dark video or song—it may be the slow seduction of your mind through a series of inputs that soften you up, that arouse a curiosity which leads only to death and darkness.

In a way, the enemy holds out supernatural "toys" like tarot cards or ouija boards or séances and says, "Just play with it ... check it out ... what can it hurt?" He doesn't tell you they are toys from hell—designed to hook you on "the other side."

Fantasy games, for example, draw the players into a "virtual" universe of curses, witchcraft, warlocks, and occult violence. "It's only a game!" somebody will object. But these games often tend to become an obsession, like all the devil's hooks ... games in which people role-play the very activities that Satan uses to rule his dark kingdom. Fantasy games often appeal to intelligent people who are drawn to the game's challenge, not to the occult connections—but as they play their roles, they exercise "powers" that copy the darkest powers of the destroyer. It is literally playing with fire.

And because we are all curious about what our future holds, your enemy needs something in his tool kit that will appeal to that curiosity. He's got it—horoscopes and psychics. You can see major celebrities promoting them on TV ... you can call a 900 number for your horoscope ... you can read yours in the newspaper ... you can find astrologers almost anywhere. It is tempting to just check it out—and maybe find out if a tall blonde is in your future—or maybe a tall fortune.

But if you stop to think about what all these predictions are based on, you might not waste the money on the 900 call. Astrology and horoscopes are based on the premise that your life is influenced by the position of the stars, and that your future can be forecast from the lineup of the stars with the constellation of your birth. Ultimately, though, a star is not some magical point of celestial light, helping to shape your future—it is a big blob of celestial gas ... a lifeless hunk of cosmic rock. Do you really believe some gas and rock millions of miles away are the key to your future?

Of course, horoscopes and psychics will be right sometimes—just like fortune cookies. If you just make some general guesses about someone's romantic or financial or educational future, you are bound to guess right about some outcomes. And besides, if the devil is using the "find out about your future" bait of horoscopes, he would certainly help an astrologer or a psychic with any information he knows about you. Their "predictions" may be right sometimes, but they are another satanic trap ... another way to get you to lift the curtain on the supernatural a little bit so he can pull you in.

Remember your enemy's strategy—just to get you to open up to the dark side of the supernatural, preferably without even knowing it is dark ... until it is too late.

Living in a world with occult possibilities everywhere you turn, you need to know how God feels about it all. He makes His feelings very clear in His Book: "Let no one be found among you who sacrifices his son or daughter in the fire, who practices divination or sorcery, interprets omens, engages in witchcraft, or casts spells, or who is a medium or spiritist or who consults the dead. Anyone who does these things is detestable to the LORD" (Deuteronomy 18:10–12).

Strong words—very strong words from God Himself. He hates every kind of occult experience or activity— contacting the spirit world, figuring out signs, tapping into psychic energy, trying to divine the future, using spiritual powers that are not from Him to make things happen. These are not supernatural toys or spooky games or innocent spiritual exploration—this is eternally serious business that crosses a line into the burning anger of God.

The simple fact is this: God has opened up His wisdom and power to those who come to Him through His Son Jesus Christ. And all non-Jesus approaches to the other side are owned by the devil. God will never be in a supernatural approach that He clearly hates—and that is any approach but Jesus. God's one and only Son bled and died to open the way for us to access the light in God's kingdom and to destroy the darkness the occult tries to explore. There is ultimately nothing there but depression, bondage, and death.

You may think you are "just looking" or "just fooling around," but there is an ugly and deadly secret about messing with Satan's stuff. When you touch any supernatural power but Jesus, you are opening yourself up to awful darkness. You are, in fact, summoning powers that want to control you. Hidden in the powers of the ouija board, the horoscope, the crystal—and hundreds of little doorways to hell—are the powers of the demonic monsters of Satan. Once you go after the evil powers they control, you are—without knowing it—opening your soul to unspeakable darkness. When they are called, they come—even if a person has no idea they have summoned the spirit world.

If you are curious about spiritual powers, take that spiritual curiosity to Jesus and His kingdom of freedom and light. After all, "He has rescued us from the dominion of darkness and brought us into the kingdom of the Son he loves, in whom we have redemption [not slavery], the forgiveness of sins" (Colossians 1:13–14). Why would you ever look back at the dark kingdom Jesus died to rescue you from?

You know now where the door marked "curiosity" goes. Lock it forever.

Deadly Door #2: Powerlessness

Satan also loves to come knocking on the door of a person who feels powerless and victimized.

Ruth (name changed) was a young woman who was raised in a dysfunctional family. The devil piqued her curiosity about occult powers with a slumber party séance when she was in sixth grade. The girls there giggled as they decided to try to make contact with one girl's dead grand-mother. They turned down the lights, joined hands, and began to talk to the "spirits" out there. It was all supposed to be fun and games. There were a few weird noises and a window shade suddenly rolled up—and that was enough for everybody except Ruth. For her, there was something exciting about this exploring the "other side." She had no idea that this curiosity would take her farther than she ever planned to go.

Ruth delved deeper and deeper into the occult until she began to practice witchcraft. As a teenage witch, she felt she had power to hurt people whom she did not like or who did not like her. If you had asked Ruth if she believed in the devil, she would have said no—"My power comes from me, not the devil." Satan rattled the door marked "powerlessness" and found a way to get a wounded girl's attention—and eventually her soul.

That power game is one your enemy would love to use on you, especially if you have a lot of hurt in your background. It is often wounded people who are the most vulnerable to an offer that says, "Hey, wouldn't you like to have a way to be in charge for a change … to have some control?" Ironically, Satan uses your being some-one's victim to ultimately make you *his* victim.

One awful night Ruth learned this truth. It suddenly became unexplainably cold in her room—and she was driven to her knees by some overwhelming dark force. It was the devil, coming to make Ruth his. She became a prisoner of the darkness that night.

Thank God, she did not remain a prisoner. Ruth met some kids in whom Jesus Christ lived—and they pointed her in the Savior's direction. One day after school, it was my privilege to introduce Ruth to the Liberator. Only Jesus could free her, and He did.

If life has been hard for you, some power may look good to you. Usually, your enemy wants you to believe that you have tapped into some inner power that is from you, not from him. You might run if you knew that the power was from hell itself. So, the devil seldom autographs his power tricks. He puts your name on them, appealing to your ego.

If you have been flirting with power from the other side, you may already be experiencing the creeping control of the destroyer. It may be a deeper depression than ever before ... more frequent bouts of depression ... anger burning higher and hotter inside ... spiritual boredom—a growing disinterest in anything about Jesus ... even self-destructive thoughts. Those are signs of an invasion from hell. And the longer you flirt with the darkness, the stronger its hold will become. But remember—there is Someone whose power to rescue you is far greater than the devil's power to hold you. Jesus is the Liberator.

If it is power you need in your life, why go with the loser? In God's words, Jesus "disarmed the powers and authorities [the devil and his demons] ... He made a public spectacle of them, triumphing over them by the cross" (Colossians 2:15). Jesus conquered what no man in history has ever been able to conquer—death. No matter how rich, how powerful, how famous a person may have been, they are in their grave tonight. But I have been to the grave of Jesus Christ—and there is nobody home! Three days after He died, Jesus Christ blew the doors off

His grave! All the powers of earth and hell could not hold the Son of God in that tomb.

That is power!

Deadly Door #3: Spiritual Vacuum

As he "prowls around looking for someone to devour," Satan looks for people who are spiritually empty and searching for some spiritual reality. Of course, he has no spiritual reality to offer them, but he can offer a spiritual package that looks like the road to God.

One car the cosmic kidnapper tries to lure you into says "New Age" on the side. There is a lot of talk about cosmic consciousness, psychic energy, the power within, Mother Earth, karma, angels, holistic healing, crystals—all focused on the same appeal as the séance and witchcraft—power. But the power is supposedly in you or in nature. It all sounds very uplifting—until you realize who is really behind the power pitch. The devil does not just come to people in evil or dark or scary packages. Sometimes he comes in the wrapping you would least expect—the bright light of spirituality. But God, who does not want you to be deceived, again blows the enemy's cover. He warns, "Satan himself masquerades as an angel of light. It is not surprising, then, if his servants masquerade as servants of righteousness" (2 Corinthians 11:14–15).

In an age when we hear a lot about "angels" and "light," isn't it interesting to discover that Satan knows how to play that game? Which means that a lot of what you hear that may sound like something very spiritual may actually be just another disguise for the destroyer. One hint is to look at the New Age section at a local bookstore—and notice what other books are in that same section ... books on the occult, black arts, and other supernatural practices that God says He hates.

This "spiritual power" pitch is really nothing new. The devil used it to spiritually seduce Adam and Eve way back in the Garden of Eden, and he has not come up with a more effective lie since. The tempter said to his very first victims, "You will not surely die [if you eat from the tree of life which God had forbidden] ... for God knows that when you eat of it your eyes will be opened, and you will be like God, knowing good and evil" (Genesis 3:5). Same appeal, same unlocked door—"you can have spiritual power without doing what God says." It was a lie then— it's a lie now. It led to death then—it leads to death now.

But if you are looking for something spiritual to fill the hole in your heart, you may have a door standing wide open for the invasion of the darkness. The devil will come to you in the "light" of New Age spirituality ... the Christian-sounding but Christ-diminishing teachings of an attractive cult ... or even in Christian religion that is very moral but missing your need for a Savior.

But the power of the crystal, the power of the cult, and the power of the Christless religion is all the same power at its source—the deceptive power of Satan him- self, designed to keep you away from Jesus.

Satan knows there is a spiritual vacuum in your heart—and he knows that Jesus is who that vacancy is designed for. But if you figure that out, he has lost you. So he has to come up with some beautiful, spiritual sub- stitutes for the real thing—a spiritual world without Christ. But his counterfeits all go the same place. "There is a way that seems right to a man, but in the end it leads to death" (Proverbs 14:12).

You will put something in the spiritual hole in your heart ... you cannot live with it empty. If you do not open the door of your heart to Jesus—the One the Bible says you were made by and made for—you will open the door to something or someone else. And right behind them will come the lying author of everything spiritual that is not Jesus—Satan, the prison master of hell.

The hole in your heart was made for Jesus—only He is big enough to fill it. He says, "Here I am! I stand at the door and knock. If anyone hears my voice and opens the door, I will come in" (Revelation 3:20).

Open the door to this One who loved you enough to die for you. Then lock the door once and for all.

10 Prime-Time Poison

Letting Garbage into Your Control Room

GIGO.

That little word started bouncing around when computers began to appear in our lives. Programmers would use it to refer to a major cause of bad data coming out of a computer—GIGO—Garbage In, Garbage Out. If you feed a computer bad input, guaranteed you will get bad output. It matters what you put in your computer.

Your life is run by a computer. No, you are not some "Star Trek" android. But what you feel, think, choose, and do is largely governed by your unique model of the most sophisticated computer in the world—the human mind. Just like your computer with its input, your mind is going to put out the kind of material you put in. And it matters what you put in your computer. Ultimately, it will show up in what you talk about, what you dream about, what you expect in relationships with the opposite sex, what you spend on, what you consider right and wrong—your life is literally being shaped by what you are programming into your mind.

Eating Ants

Chocolate-covered ants. How many would you like? I think I'll just pass on this particular treat. There actually are such things as chocolate-covered ants, but most people do not ever plan to munch an ant. The only way you could get them to eat an ant would be to cover it with chocolate and not tell them what is inside.

The devil knows that is his best strategy for getting life-wrecking ideas into your life—cover it with "chocolate" and cover up what is inside. Except it is not insects your enemy has concealed in nice-tasting packages—it's poison. Soul poison.

His method for infecting your future starts by infecting your mind, the central command center of your choices. The evil strategy by which your enemy works is frighteningly simple ...

THINK IT → WANT IT → DO IT → PAY FOR IT!

Satan is much too smart to tell you where he is ultimately planning to take you. So, he starts by just trying to get you to think about something that is wrong. "Hey, I'm not asking you to do anything wrong—just enjoy this thought for a minute!"—that is his subtle approach. And, of course, he will be so invisible that it will never even occur to you that anything dark is going on.

But once the dark thought has been allowed access into your control room, the hijacking of your heart is under way. "Think it" becomes "want it"—not only a thought about something wrong, but a desire for it. God makes sure we know where it goes from there ... "After desire has conceived, it gives birth to sin; and sin, when it is full-grown, gives birth to death" (James 1:15).

Once you have a desire for something we were never meant to do, all your enemy has to do is provide an attractive opportunity for you to take the next step—do it. That is desire giving birth to sin—exactly what God said would happen. And the next step He predicted will happen, too—sin "gives birth to death." That does not mean you will suddenly fall over dead ... but it does mean that sin will kill a lot of things that matter to you. And Satan will be laughing as he watches you pay for it. And it all begins with a thought, a lie about some part of life where your enemy wants to set you up for hurt and regret.

But how does the devil get people to open up their control room to the thoughts that can do so much damage? Remember the chocolate-covered ants? He has to wrap up his lies in something that really looks and tastes good.

Think about it: "If I wanted to get a lot of people to buy a loser product, I would make it popular—something a lot of people, including a lot of cool people, are into, make it exciting—a product that makes you feel as if you are really missing something if you are not into it, make it everywhere—an idea that keeps showing up everywhere you turn."

And how do ideas get popular, exciting, and everywhere in our world today? Through media, of course. TV, music, radio, videos, books, magazines, star endorsements, humor—twenty-four hours a day, seven days a week, messages of every kind are bombarding our brains. And planting thoughts ... sneaking into our control room. If someone wants to get us thinking about their product, they introduce it through what we watch and listen to all day.

Your enemy knows that. So he has laced all those messages we get with his poisonous lies. And you can be sure that if the devil wants to set us up with a "think it," he will put it in a very bright, very attractive package. If the devil has his lies hidden in a TV program, it will be a show that is very clever, very popular—something "everybody's watching."

If he is peddling his poison in a song, you can bet it will be in a tune that you cannot get out of your head— maybe reinforced with a music video that puts a picture with the lie. The devil's deadly ideas will be in the slick- est magazines, played on the coolest stations, portrayed in the trendiest programs, and talked about by the biggest stars. Pretty soon it seems as if all your friends are watching or listening to this exciting package that has a message from hell inside—and you feel really "out of it" if you aren't into it! The devil is selling prime-time poison!

Which means that "entertainment" is a lot more than entertainment. It is about ideas and lifestyles and values being pounded into your brain around the clock. And, of course, the devil wants to sneak his lies in at a time when your mind is on cruise control—those lazy moments when we aren't thinking about what we're thinking about. Like the time we watch TV, listen to our music, lis- ten to the radio, get a few laughs.

This strategy for your spiritual seduction calls for a strong counterattack if you do not want the hijacker from hell in your control room. That counterattack is laid out very simply by the God who loves you … "Above all else, guard your heart, for it is the wellspring of life" (Proverbs 4:23). God says to station a security force around the control room of your heart and mind. Monitor what gets into your heart, be very careful about what gets into your control room.

The plan to "devour" you begins with feeding the dark side of you—the desires for sex too soon, the anger, the depressing thoughts, the rebellion against any boundaries, the temptation to party with alcohol or drugs, the sarcasm and cynicism, the urge to do "anything for love." If Satan can fuel those desires, he can eventually take you over with one or more of them.

So, the logical place to fight a dark takeover is when it is small—when it is only an idea. It is much more difficult to resist the darkness when it has moved to "want it" or "do it". The one sure way to protect yourself from the destructive plans Satan has for you is to keep out wrong thoughts in the first place—to guard your heart!

So instead of just "vegging out" mentally for a movie, TV show, music, or magazine, decide to watch what you are watching and screen what you are listening to. You cannot afford to let a hijacker sneak into your control room, even in a cool disguise.

Four Hijackers

In the military, when a sentry falls asleep on guard duty, he is in big trouble! He should be—when the guard is not guarding, anything can get in!

Your enemy, who wants to plant his time bombs in your brain, knows he can do his best work when your "guard" is asleep. He has four favorite ways to soften you up, to make sure you are not thinking about what you're doing, and to plant ideas and choices that will ultimately destroy you. They are his "hijackers."

Hijacker #1: Entertainment

You want to take a mental time-out or a "getaway trip"—so you kick back with a movie or TV, with music or something to read. If you were the devil, wouldn't you slip your ideas into that "entertainment"? He does! And we end up watching and listening to things that portray, promote, or suggest lifestyles that we would never allow someone to do in our living room. But because it is "numb-brain" time, we open ourselves up to the invasion of thoughts Satan plans to use against us. Without even realizing it, we are soon accepting ideas and activities that we once had no place for. It is like the artillery bombardments that almost always precede a full-scale military invasion—they soften up the ones you are about to attack so it is easier to conquer them.

Hijacker #2: Alcohol

Drinking and "good times" are almost synonymous for a lot of young people—the good times begin when the booze arrives. Part of the appeal of drinking is that it "loosens you up" ... you do things you would never do otherwise ... things you sometimes cannot even remember doing. But the bill still comes whether you remember what you were doing or not. The lie is that "I was drinking last night ... I couldn't help what I was doing." You could help drinking in the first place. God's "videocam" and the "consequences bill" are still running, whether you can feel anything or not! The devil loves it when you drink … you are giving him one of his best openings to plant his poison in your life.

The alcohol commercials that show beautiful people having beautiful times in beautiful places are not telling the ugly truth about their product. When my kids and I saw those commercials on TV, we sometimes thought up our own "whole truth" commercials. How about a bleeding man being pulled out of the wreckage of the car he just totaled because he was drunk? Or a man storming in the house drunk and slapping his little daughter across the room? "Good times?"

God reveals the ugly truth about alcohol in this straight talk from His Book. "Who has woe? Who has sorrow? Who has strife? Who has complaints? Who has needless bruises? Who has bloodshot eyes? Those who linger over wine.… Do not gaze at wine when it is red, when it sparkles in the cup, when it goes down smoothly! In the end, it bites like a snake and poisons like a viper. Your eyes will see strange sights and your mind imagine confusing things. You will be like one sleeping on the high seas, lying on top of the rigging. 'They hit me,' you will say, 'but I'm not hurt! They beat me, but I don't feel it! When will I wake up so I can find another drink?'" (Proverbs 23:29–35).

Alcohol promises so much "fun" and delivers so much destruction. It "bites," and it "poisons." Since it puts your common sense and your conscience to sleep, alcohol is one of Satan's most successful life hijackers.

Hijacker #3: Drugs

Besides entertainment and alcohol, your enemy knows the power of drugs to immobilize your mind and do what he wants there. In some ways, the effect of drugs is similar to alcohol in its numbing of your brain and your heart. Drugs can also produce a feeling of "I just don't care"—a feeling Satan is hoping he can bring you to. When you "don't care," he can manipulate you into doing things that will cost you what you never expected to pay. With both alcohol and drugs, the issue is losing control—which sets you up for the one who wants to take control of your life and your future.

Hijacker #4: Pornography

If your enemy can plant twisted sexual images in your mind, he has a powerful way to make you a slave, make you ashamed, and make you mess up sex. So he bombards you with images of barely clothed or unclothed people and of steamy sexual situations. The devil's goal is to hijack your passions and make them his. He wants to make it impossible for you to think about the opposite sex with respect and purity ... to corrupt the beauty of sex with your lifetime love ... to set you up for dirty choices you once thought you would never make. Pornography is strongly addicting—once you have opened up your heart to it, it is as if you can never get enough of the perversion.

Knowing the destructive power of sexual fantasies, the biblical leader Job said, "I made a covenant with my eyes not to look lustfully at a girl" (Job 31:1). Any young man or woman who wants to keep satanic poison out of their mind needs to step up to a commitment just like that. And even if you may be hooked by hell's fantasies, there is a Rescuer who has the power to restore your control room. "We take captive every thought to make it obedient to Christ" (2 Corinthians 10:5). The same Savior who had the power to conquer death on Easter morning also has the power to liberate you from porno-slavery ... to make every thought obey Him!

Finally, there's a hijacker so powerful that we need to explore it in more detail. That mental hijacker is—you guessed it—music.

Bait with a Beat

No fish is going to swim up to a bare hook and take a bite of something that could do him serious damage. But fish do end up on hooks a lot—because somebody puts attractive bait (at least to a fish) on his hook. The enemy who wants to hook you knows he cannot just throw his bare hook out there—he has to present his lies to you wrapped in bait you will bite on. Then, like the fish jumping around in the fisherman's bucket, it will be too late when you finally realize what you bit on.

There is no more powerful bait in Satan's "capture your mind" tool kit than music. Not all music, but music that carries lies, feelings, and ideas he wants in your head and heart.

Music has never been so important to any generation as it is today. Someone quoted to me a strong statement from one of America's most famous rock lead singers— "When I was in high school, my music was my best friend." For a lot of young people, their music is much more than tunes—it is a part of who they are and even how they cope. A study was done asking teenagers what they do when they are going through hard times—they ranked fifty-three different options for "coping" with pressure and problems. Talking to Mom or Dad ranked near the bottom of their choices. Talking to friends ranked near the top. But the number one way teenagers said they were handling their hassles was "my music."

Your music is there for you in your up times, your down times, your romantic times, your lonely times, your spiritual times, your rowdy times, your quiet times. You can't always find a friend to talk to, but you can almost always have your music to listen to—on your radio, your Walkman, your tapes or CDs, or on MTV. Your music is all over your life—which makes it very important, based on how many hours it is filling your mind each week. Obviously, you don't sit there lost in Walkmanland saying, "Whadayaknow—I'm being influenced right now!" You don't feel it ... but you are being influenced. With your guard down. With the possibility of garbage dancing right into your control room.

"Don't get on my case about my music," you might object. "I just like the beat—I don't even listen to the lyrics!" And Junior Fish said to Mama Fish, "Don't get on my case about fishhooks! I just like the taste of worms—I don't get near fishhooks!" Inside the bait—or the beat—may be a hook you do not want to think about. And I honestly have no desire to "get on your case about your music"—I just want you to be able to recognize deadly hooks in disguise. But I do not buy the idea that "the lyrics don't matter to me."

Music carries messages. Why do you think advertisers pay big bucks to have somebody write a jingle for a commercial? Because music is a hammer that pounds ideas into your head. I know that United Airlines has the "friendly skies," and that "the best part of waking up" is Folger's in your cup, and that Chevy trucks are "like a rock"—because they drove those ideas into my head with music.

You cannot repeatedly listen to music without picking up the messages it carries. Do you think the slickest, sickest salesman in the universe would not plant his messages in some of the hottest music of the day? To deny that is to hand the keys of your control room to the one who wants to destroy you.

It is naive—and dangerous—to say, "It doesn't matter what music I listen to." It matters a lot! Music is just too powerful for you to listen to a song just because "I like it"—no matter what the style of music. Satan has planted his life-wrecking lies in every style of music—rock, country, alternative, rap, easy listening, metal—the devil speaks every musical language, except music that praises and worships God. So, no matter what your musical tastes, it is important that you have some boundaries around your music. The question is, "When is music out-of-bounds?" Here are some practical ways to evaluate when your music has gone too far.

Music Is Out-of-Bounds When It Is a Wall

When music becomes so important that it puts a wall between you and your parents or other key people in your life, it has become too important. And it is definitely out-of-bounds.

Music Is Out-of-Bounds When It Is Poison

When I have a cold, and my nose is at flood stage, I take one of those little pills that promises quick relief. In a little while, the Kleenex 911 alert is over.

But now I have another problem. The nose is dry, but now the eyes are drooping with sudden sleepiness. The pill made me feel better, but it had a side effect that could make me drive into a telephone pole! You have to think about the effect something is going to have, not just how good it might make you feel.

That surely applies to music. If you want to avoid your enemy's mind infiltration, you need to ask, "What effect does this music really have on me?" The issue here, though, is not just getting sleepy ... it is getting poisoned mentally, emotionally, and spiritually. Knowing that Satan wants to take over the control room of our mind, God tells us how to keep him out ... "Be wise about what is good, and innocent about what is evil. The God of peace will soon crush Satan under your feet" (Romans 16:19–20).

Part of the victory plan for crushing Satan is to fill up on what is good and shut out what is "evil." But how can you tell if music is having a slow, poisoning effect on you? Try honestly answering these questions:

1. Does this music feed my dark side, or does it bring out the best in me?

In high school, our son Doug dared to think about the music he was listening to—and he made a gutsy decision to make some changes. Later, he described the impact of that change. He said, "When I listened to harder music, I was harder; since I've started to focus on Christian music, I've become softer and more caring as a person." Doug had discovered that the side of you that you feed is the side of you that will grow. Could it be that some of the music you have been listening to is feeding your dark side—the anger, the depression, the rebellion, the loneliness, the "I don't care" attitude, the withdrawing into yourself? If it is, it is slowly poisoning you.

Maybe the music you listen to doesn't carry many dark messages. But it could lure you into something more damaging. Satan would love to hook you on a musical package, then pull you into garbage that comes in that package.

Knowing how important your control room is, God provides a simple test for measuring what is going into your mind ... "Whatever is true, whatever is noble, whatever is right, whatever is pure, whatever is lovely, whatever is admirable—if anything is excellent or praiseworthy—think about such things" (Philippians 4:8).

Put your music next to those words—does it fit? If not, you do not need it in the control center of your life.

2. *Does this music present or promote what God is against?*

If so, then it is definitely out-of-bounds! Music that describes or glorifies sex outside of marriage, irreverence toward God or Jesus, the dark side of the supernatural, doing whatever you feel like doing—that kind of music is soul-poison, designed to pull you into the danger zone.

Music Is Out-of-Bounds When It Is a Locked Door

"My music is my business!" Which means "I don't want anyone telling me anything about my music!" If you have decided not to accept any critique of what you are listening to, you have closed your mind and your heart.

Music has become too important when it is a part of you that you refuse to evaluate or pass judgment on. In fact, it may have even become what the Bible calls an "idol"—something that has become bigger to you than God is. In your heart you may even be saying, "God, I don't even want You to mess with my music." Hello, idol worship. You have let your music become a "stronghold" that "sets itself up against the knowledge of God" (2 Corinthians 10:5). The Bible leaves no doubt as to what we are to do with "strongholds" where we have hung out a "No trespassing" sign—we need to "demolish strongholds" (2 Corinthians 10:4).

Music Is Out-of-Bounds When It Is Your Answer

Something is out of line when listening to music is teenagers' number one choice for dealing with their problems. Music might comfort you—but music can't love you, solve your problem, or meet your need. Only people can do that. People like a mother, a father, a counselor, a pastor. And music may turn out to be more of an anesthetic that only masks the pain that is killing you inside. If you use music as a frequent pain reliever, it may only keep you from going where you could find a cure. Music is there for us in our moments of need, but it can never remove the "Vacancy" sign on your heart.

For Kurt Cobain, the lead singer of Nirvana, music was pretty much his life. But apparently, even when he was at the top of his game musically, music was not enough reason to keep living. His pain must have finally overtaken him—he took his own life. The music stopped forever. I only wish Kurt Cobain could have experienced the life-changing love of Jesus Christ. Only Jesus can fill the vacancy in the human heart—because it is God-sized. No music, no musician, no earth-person can possibly fill it. When you bring your deepest needs to the Lord, He gives you something better than temporary relief ... He gives you a rescue.

David was the best-known musician of his day, but like Kurt Cobain, he knew what it was to hit emotional bottom. But there he found a reason to live, not a reason to die. He said in his personal journal, recorded in the Bible: "[The Lord] heard my cry ... [and] lifted me out of the slimy pit, out of the of the mud and mire; he set my feet on a rock and gave me a firm place to stand. He put a new song in my mouth ..." (Psalm 40:1-3).

Music might make you feel a little better in your pit, but it cannot "lift you out." Only the Savior can do that. And instead of just changing your feelings for a little while, He can change your life forever—and give you, for the first time in your life, "a firm place to stand."

The Antivirus Program

Not long ago, someone in our office turned on their computer and found an unexpected greeting on the screen—"Warning: This computer has been infected with the 'stoned' virus." We called our computer serviceman and he basically said, "Freeze!" This was a deadly new program that could cause a meltdown in our computer hard drive.

Man, am I glad there are anti-infection, virus-scanning programs! It was one of those programs that saved us the day our computer almost got very sick from the "stoned virus." Because there are so many viruses out there that can ruin everything, you really need to defend yourself against the invasion.

The computer that controls you—your mind—needs the same kind of protection. You have an enemy—a powerful enemy—who is bombarding your system with spiritual viruses. Because God made you and loves you, the devil wants you to crash. Many people have crashed because they did not take the attack of the killer viruses seriously. They were not careful about what got into their computer.

Long before computers were thought of, God was warning us to keep Satan's spiritual infection out of our control room—"Above all else, guard your heart, for it is the wellspring of life." The antivirus program that keeps out the enemy's invasion carries these instructions:

Decide That What Happens in Your Control Room Really Matters

Unless you realize that your mind and heart are the battleground on which the outcomes of your life will be decided, you will never fight to protect it.

Remove Any Infectious Material That You Have

If there are things you watch or listen to that are feeding your dark side, do what you are supposed to do with garbage—get rid of it. Don't hang onto it until it smells and you have rats in the house! There may be music, magazines, books, or videos that you need to destroy—

even if they are some favorites of yours. They have pol-
luted your control room long enough—they have to go
before they spread more infection. In God's words, "Let us
throw off everything that hinders and the sin that so easily entangles" (Hebrews 12:1).

Clean Out Your Control Room Every Morning

Before any other influence starts programming you
for the day, spend time with Jesus. Listen to His "voice"
as He prepares you for your day, using His words in the
Bible. And ask Him to forgive and clean up any junk you
allowed in during the last twenty-four hours.

Load Up on Good Input

It is important that you fill up your mind with positive music, videos, and magazines. What you put in your
mind is important, not just what you keep out. Just as
with physical food, you do not just avoid what will cause
damage—you eat the things that are good for you, too.
Remember, what you eat affects you later. That goes for
the "food" that builds you up, too.

Turn Over the Controls to the Commander-in-Chief

If you are serious about your life being the most it
can be, why not turn it over to the One who can do the
most with it—Jesus Christ! And since almost everything
you do begins in the control room of your mind and
heart, His leadership needs to start there. All of us already
have piles of garbage accumulated in our heart from all
the dark inputs we have taken in over the years. And
they are poisoning our attitudes and actions over and

over again. That is why Jesus invites us to an exciting new beginning—a miraculous transplant, in a way. "Offer your bodies as living sacrifices, holy and pleasing to God.... Do not conform any longer to the pattern of this world, but be transformed by the renewing of your mind" (Romans 12:1–2).

Something amazing happens when you bring down the flag that has flown over your control room—the flag with your name on it—and you raise the flag that says "Jesus" on it. He begins a miracle process of cleaning out the garbage of the past and replacing thoughts from hell with thoughts from heaven. Jesus totally renews, rewires, and refocuses the control room in your heart so you can become a person with little to regret and much to give.

Everything that matters begins in your control room. You have no more important decision to make than who will run it and what you will allow to enter it. The hijacker from hell knocks on the door with his life-wrecking darkness in disguise. The Liberator from heaven knocks on the door with His life-changing truth and light. As the control room goes, so goes the rest of your life.

No matter what time bomb might be ticking in your life, your Creator is the only One who can ultimately defuse it. If you would like to know more about beginning a personal relationship with Jesus Christ, I would love to hear from you. The address is:

Ron Hutchcraft
P.O. Box 1818
Wayne, NJ 07474–1818

Ron Hutchcraft

*G*od didn't put us here to make money, friends, grades, or a team. He put us here to make a difference!"

Ron Hutchcraft is an international speaker, radio host, and author. His radio broadcast "Alive! with Ron Hutchcraft!" is a high-energy youth program that features humor, drama, contemporary music, a teenage studio audience, and biblical straight talk about issues facing young people today: relationships, loneliness, suicide, parents, peer pressure, and more. "Alive!" is heard each week across the USA and overseas, including over the Armed Forces Radio Network. A Spanish version of "Alive!" called "Chévere!" is heard in Latin America. People of all ages enjoy "Alive!"

Ron has spoken across North America and Europe, the United Kingdom, South America, Africa, Asia, the South Pacific, and the West Indies. He has spoken at numerous youth events, conferences, and college campuses on "Looking for love in all the right places" and "How to have lasting relationships in a breakable world."

He coauthored *Letters from the College Front* (girls' and guys' editions), which gives practical advice to college-bound high school students. He is also the host of the video "Sex at Its Best: A Positive Morality for Today's Youth."

Ron also works among and with Native American young people on reservations across North America. In the summer, he travels with "On Eagles' Wings," which he founded. "On Eagles' Wings" is a leadership development team of Native Americans ages 16–35.

OTHER COOL STUFF FOR YOUNG PEOPLE

FROM RON HUTCHCRAFT

Internet: "Alive! with Ron Hutchcraft" is the Make A Difference web site for today's youth! At www.hutchcraft.com, you'll find "Real Life, Real Answers," real audio clips, and much more! Check it out! Lots of stuff for adults, too! (Ron Hutchcraft Ministries is a part of the Gospel Communications Network, www.gospelcom.net.)

Video: "Sex at Its Best! A Positive Morality for Today's Youth"

A high-energy, fast-moving video, designed to present today's youth with a life-changing, love-saving challenge, with a plan for "how to keep sex special." But more significantly, Ron presents an opportunity for young people to surrender their lives to Jesus Christ. This video is a great supplement to the material presented in chapter one of this book. Leader's Guide included. Available at your local Christian bookstore, or call Gospel Films, (800) 253-0413.

Radio Broadcast: "Alive! with Ron Hutchcraft!"

This weekly, one-hour program features issues young people care about, a live studio audience of teenagers, contemporary Christian music, drama, and biblical straight talk that hits home. To find out how you can hear "Alive! with Ron Hutchcraft," contact your local Christian radio station, or Ron Hutchcraft Ministries, P.O. Box 1818, Wayne, NJ 07474, (973) 696–2161, rhm@gospelcom.net.

Book: *Letters from the College Front*

Guys' Edition by Ron Hutchcraft & Doug Hutchcraft (his son) *Girls' Edition* by Ron Hutchcraft & Lisa Hutchcraft Whitmer (his daughter)

Headed to college? Letters straight from college—from the "front"—in which high school graduates will find helpful advice, biblical principles, and straightforward discussion on important issues and situations related to college life. Available at your local Christian bookstore, or call Baker Book House, (800) 877–2665.

For Youth Workers and Parents

Book: *The Battle for a Generation: Capturing the Hearts of Our Youth*

Want to help make a difference in the lives of today's young people? This book provides knowledge, practical methods, and a vision for reaching today's generation for Jesus Christ. Combining plenty of illustrations and examples of effective methods, this book gives an up close look at the world of today's teenager. Available at your local Christian bookstore, or call Moody Press, (800) 678–6928.

Evangelism Booklet: *Yours for Life*

In this minibooklet, Ron presents the core Gospel message of Jesus Christ in nonreligious language. An ideal, contemporary witnessing tool for all ages. Available at your local Christian bookstore, or contact American Tract Society, (800) 548–7228

For Parents

Book, Cassette, Video: *5 Needs Your Child Must Have Met at Home*

A practical strategy for meeting the unique challenges of parenting today. Parents of all ages will find a road map for how to raise stable children in an unstable world. Also, parents will be introduced to the importance of a relationship with Jesus Christ. Available at your local Christian bookstore, or call Zondervan, (800) 727-3480 (for book or audio pages), or Gospel Films, (800) 253-0413 (for video).

For further information, please contact:

Ron Hutchcraft Ministries, Inc.
P.O. Box 1818
Wayne, NJ 07474-1818
973-696-2161
FAX: 973-694-1182
INTERNET: www.hutchcraft.com
e-mail: rhm@gospelcom.net

We want to hear from you. Please send your comments about this
book to us in care of the address below. Thank you.

GRAND RAPIDS, MICHIGAN 49530
www.zondervan.com